THE SHEPHERD'S SEAT

A Prophetic Guide to Holiness

EXPERIENCE

DR. MELVA DORSEY

Order this book online at www.trafford.com
or email orders@trafford.com

Most Trafford titles are also available at major online book retailers.

Printed in the United States of America.

ISBN: 978-1-4269-0882-8 (sc)

Trafford rev. 06/04/2012

 www.trafford.com

North America & international
toll-free: 1 888 232 4444 (USA & Canada)
phone: 250 383 6864 ♦ fax: 812 355 4082

ITNOJ

Praises of the Virtue of
The Shepherd Seat Experience
Prophetic Guide to Holiness

"Dr. Melva Dorsey speaks biblical truths which awaken our spirits to see what others seem somehow to be missing. If you are tough-minded, you will come away with clear thinking and knowing there is a better way. You will become more courageous to stand against the enemy and just worship God.

Dr. Dorsey pours her heart out in an abundance of love towards you, to show the one-way, truth and life to live (1 John 14:6.). "The Shepherd Seat Experience," instructs us on how to press toward the mark of the high calling through worship; things may be hard times, but there is purpose in glorifying God.

God has truly ordained this woman of God to excel with spiritual insight that is amazing as she paints pictures with her prophetic eye. In addition, the faith she has shown of the greater works to come has been portrayed throughout this book. She is a divinely chosen ripen fruit for such a time as this and you will believe the Lord is her Shepherd. This book truly shows the way to Holiness and inspires us to reach it. Dr. Dorsey sees right into our heart and does the work of a skilled surgeon operating on our heart to learn to worship.

Be honest with yourselves we are not where we need to be in Christ, yet. I repent and go forward to the "spa of forgiveness" and the love pouring out the oil of our salvation upon our souls with the peace that Dr Dorsey talks about in this book. Listen to the things this beautiful woman of many colors is speaking from God, He is helping us to enter into His Glory at the point worshipping Christ."

God Bless!
Pastor Sharlene Rodgers
Family Affair Keepers Ministries,
Cleveland, Ohio

Another says…

"I enjoyed reading The Shepherd's Seat Experience. I related to it... giving the many experiences that occurred to people in the bible and relating those concepts to many of our situations of today and God is the same yesterday, today and tomorrow.

Not only does Apostle Melva Dorsey relate to the fear we have in moving into our destiny of ministry, she also relates to how we can be misjudged and hurt, even by church folk. This book reveals that we will go through many things in life, but if we stay in Christ Jesus who will never leave us nor forsake us, we have the victory in all things.

God bless you for all the work you do...

Minster Shirley Harrell,
Rehoboth Apostolic Outreach Ministry,
Cleveland, Ohio

CONTENTS

CONTENTS cont.

INTRODUCTION

"Therefore do not be unwise, but understand what the will of the Lord is" (Ephesians 5:17).

The Shepherd's Seat Experience Prophetic Guide to Holiness pages are filled with divine revelations to the will of God. God has not called us to the door of the Holy Place to graze from afar; He has called us into His presence to make our enemies His footstool. God will lift us up into His lap where we will find the comfort of knowing our Lord for ourselves.

Trusting that God hears our silent tears and is waiting to bless us, we are assured all will be well. The majestic voice of the Lord is speaking to our hearts. He loves us and is in pursuit of all those who have an ear to hear these revelations.

Being in alignment with the will of God, we rise from the darkness of our loathed selves to depict a "perfected" picture of order and the death of our flesh. Choosing God's will is the only way into the lap of the Lord's presence in holiness. No woman or man has the power to stand firmly in his or her own feebleness without God. God is sounding a trumpet so we will be as He created us... *in His image.*

We should thirst after His presence and become unrecognizable in any way of our loathsome selves; our desire should be that *only* He might be seen in all our associations. Becoming one with our Creator sends us back into the hands that designed us and should be our ultimate quest.

The Shepherd's Seat Experience, teaches us to go boldly into the Holy of Holies, unafraid knowing that our ABBA is there. Where else can we go? Only to our Father who has place Himself as a fortress within us. The Holy Spirit is our refuge against all our fears and doubts of this world.

In His presence, we will not give His glory or His praise to any graven image. Our lives are humbled before Him simply for the joy of living emptied and surrendered in His lap. As we witness the unfolding of *The Shepherd's*

Seat Experience in our lives, we begin to worship God for God's pleasure. Christians are equipped to meet God's expectations to find a new facet of life in their walk.

These guidelines teach the benefits of holiness that we may forever do away with self-will and honor God's will. We are inspired by our faith, and God is pleased as we obey and we receive healing and deliverance. The Lord brought us to this moment to receive the greatest gift any soul can attain, which is to find the heart of God.

The Shepherd's Seat Experience predisposes us to live the Prophetic lives that God has ordained. We are far from understanding this conceptual framework of the creation evidence by our disobedience. We violently despise the will of God by ignoring His divine patterns connected to His principles!

There is more to it than just being saved, we have work to do. We are locked into a place where the only escape is God's way, which leads us to eternal life. The Words *"And God Said"* are the most powerful words ever uttered. We are held in the mouth of God's spoken Word, which He sends forth to multiply within us. Our Prophetic lives have been hand carved by the King of kings who is always at the door of our lives seeking entry. God is Holy therefore; He wants us to be Holy like Him and in His spiritual image. God is not looking for His "face" but *He is looking for our hearts to be like His* when He returns.

There is a worldwide urgency in the atmosphere as time is passing us by unnoticed. Look around and see if you do not agree that things are moving at an accelerated pace. This is the time when all things are being called back into the mouth of God. He has revealed the Bible to us and we must realize that *He said it and it is truth.*

The requests made by the living God who neither sleeps nor slumbers is always victorious. God said that we are His alone and that He is a jealous God. God does not envy any material thing we have, remember He spoke and made it all for us to enjoy. God is jealous because we have not learned to worship Him in Spirit and in Truth. We have not drawn close enough to seek His Kingdom and righteousness for our well-being.

The Shepherd's Seat Experience Prophetic truths train us how to live, move, and have our being in God. Despite what our self-will says, man cannot live by bread alone, but every Word that proceeds out of the mouth of God! Did you know that you are God's spoken "Word" made flesh? Just like Jesus Christ, we are bound to live for God. Yes, we walk in the glory of the Lord on a daily basis and still think we are our own. We are not our own, God have purchased us with *"the precious blood"* of Jesus.

I hope that as you read the pages of *The Shepherd's Seat Experience,* you will receive a glimpse of the Glory of God as I did and you will never be the same. Come now let us reason together, God is looking throughout the earth to bless someone and He wants it to be you.

Salvation is a free ride waiting to pick you up where you are and take you to places you have never known. These places are hidden within you to realize that *God is our Creator.* We are created in His image to be righteous in all our ways and holy in all our acts just like Him. As you walk in the Spirit of *The Shepherd's Seat Experience*

Prophetic guidance, you will see Him; hear Him; touch Him; love Him and believe Him like you have never done before. This is your season to grow in the grace and the knowledge of the Lord Jesus Christ. Understand that by looking through the eyes of God you will attain the meaning of *The Shepherd Seat Experience.*

It would be well for you to take heed and walk worthy of your calling because you are what God says one way or the other. As for me, and my house, we choose to worship God in *the beauty of holiness!*

God Bless You!

Apostle and Prophet of God Dr. Melva Dorsey,
Founder of Living Waters World Ministries,
Cleveland, Ohio

I

FOR£V£R

I pray that God will release the power of His authority over my whole being and that I will be equipped to expound on the things of His perfect will. I have no strength or thought for doing this work and I am exclusively depending on the power of His Holy Spirit. I have entered into a place of rest out from the valley, moving onto a high mountain, pushing up the clouds of my destination.

I await the Lord's arrival, trusting Him by faith and believing that He will soon come. God told me personally, *"I will never leave thee nor forsake thee" (Hebrew 13:5);* I believe Him. Therefore, I wait on the God of my salvation.

Rhema Revelations quickens my spirit and the peace that surpasses all understanding comforts me. This position is one of separation, but not loneliness, solitude, but not isolation. Chosen to wait on God, I lift my soul to Him. The Lord is here. I feel His presence and I can detect the fragrance of His holiness in the unseen clean and lovely excellence binding my nostrils. My eyes are ever towards the Lord and He is directing my path by His mercy and truth.

God is here to keep His covenant and His testimonies to teach me in the way He chooses with integrity, *"For the mountains shall depart, and the hills be removed; but my kindness shall not depart from thee, neither shall the covenant of my peace be removed, saith the Lord that hath mercy on thee" (Isaiah 54:10).* I expect the King of Glory to touch my heart, awaken new affections for Him, so that I may proclaim with a voice of victory and tell all of His precious promises.

What a magnificent place of restoration, renewal and recovery. The Lord brought me here to restore my soul, *"Hast thou not known? Hast thou not heard that the Everlasting God, the Lord, the Creator of the ends of the earth, faint not and neither is weary? There is no searching of His understanding. He gives power to the faint; and to them that have no might He increases strength. Even the youths shall faint and be weary, and the young men shall utterly fail; But they that wait upon the Lord shall renew their strength; they shall mount up with wings as eagles; they shall run, and not be weary; and they shall walk, and not faint" (Isaiah 40:28-31).* My experience is unfathomable; I will never comprehend how I could be so full and empty during the same time. God's love has caused the old skins of sin within me to fall away to recover my righteousness. God is the "Forever" in my life, the source of all my strength.

I am filled with His Holy Spirit; emptied of myself and set apart for His glory. My logic is humbled and pushed away to blindly trust God's purpose for my existence. Intellect is invisible in the spirit.

The Holy Spirit is guiding me to leave matters that concern the Lord to His wisdom and not to my own understanding, *"And He said unto me, my grace is sufficient for thee: for my strength is made perfect in weakness. Most gladly therefore will I rather glory in my infirmities, that the power of Christ may rest upon me. Therefore I take pleasure in infirmities, in reproaches, in necessities, in persecutions, in distresses for Christ's sake: for when I am weak, then am*

I strong" (II Corinthians 12:9-10). For a little while, I must tarry here by faith and under God's grace until "For*ever*" comes; therefore, my heart is encouraged.

Spoken oracles of wisdom strengthened me through the storms of life. He said *"Howbeit when He the Spirit of Truth, is come, He will guide you into all truth: for He shall not speak of himself but whatsoever He shall hear, that shall He speak: and He will show you things to come"(John 16:13)*. At the same time, as I waited in this resting place, the experience of God's presence and manifested glory appeared.

A whirling wind seemingly brought forth beautiful white lights with bursts of amber, blue and pink, which suddenly illuminated the area above my head. The lights magnified as they moved together and encapsulated my whole being with peace. The eternal "Now" became evident, and God's love settled all my desires and burned my soul with divine ecstasy, fulfilling my every need. Beholding God's supreme majesty, I was subdued by the wealth of His presence without an inkling of any inkling. The joyful embrace of God's glory caressed my spirit, lifting me up into His awe, marveling at His countenance. The intensity of His love was inescapable and I perceived only Him as my God, the Father of lights and giver of all good gifts.

Now, with the highest regard, my heart falls deeper in the unspeakable joy of the love of the Holy One. Beholding His glorious love, melting into the fire of truth and holy companionship, I fell down before Him to establish my worship at His feet, in honor and reverence of the sovereign power of El Shaddai, the Almighty God.

Who can stand in the revelation of Jehovah Nissi, the God who goes before us and makes the crooked places straight and not fall in His glory? The "quiet" silenced me, and until God releases my tongue, I have no voice only ears to hear. The message is becoming clearer. I hear God speaking to me. "I have brought you here to teach you who I AM." God's voice shook the foundation of my humility, no flesh can glory in His presence; the Lord acts freely and as He wills; *"Come unto me, all ye that labor and are heavy laden and I will give you rest. Take my yoke upon you and learn of me; for I am meek and lowly in heart: And ye shall find rest for your souls" (Matthew 11:28-29)."I will instruct thee and teach thee in the way which thou shall go: I will guide thee with mine eye" (Psalm 32:8).*

I know His voice and He said to me "I have always called you to this place of grace and rest; trust me and believe that you have been here before." I could not remember ever being in this place. I dared not lean on my own understanding and I trusted Him by His words.

"The reason you do not remember is because I must bring things to your remembrance in due season." *"Therefore if any man be in Christ, he is a new creature: old things are passed away; behold all things have become new" (II Corinthians 5:17).*

Wisdom spoke to me again and I press on towards the mark of the high calling never looking behind me. "You have a new assignment which is to learn everything about WHO I AM and how to worship me. You have been predestined to grow in the knowledge of my ways, my will and my word; you are my elect. It is time for you to go to another level of spiritual awareness. Let me show you these things of your journey in me" said God. My lips moved in His glory, "Which way should I go?" I replied in the fullness of my humanity?"

The Lord himself responded lovingly, *"I am the way, the truth and the life" (John 14:6).* "Will you trust me to show you who I am?" Humbled by His glory, my answer was "Yes Lord, with gladness!" I wanted to see His face, but all I could see was the awesome lights. The glory of the Lord was upon me and His love was more than enough.

The lights opened into an even brighter sphere and went before me as a guide for*ever.* I trusted God and knew I could never be alone nor forsaken and that "forever" was coming for me soon...*for yours is the Kingdom and the power and glory forever"(Matthews (6:13).*

My life is marked for glory by the eyes of the Living God established in the beginning *"Thy Word is a lamp unto my feet and a light unto my path" (Psalm 119:105).* I heard voices softly rejoicing from inside an opened gate in front of me; I perceived love, acceptance and perfect peace.

God's opened hand is the beautiful gate and He welcomed me in closer to establish me with a greater measure of faith. I realized that my growth in the knowledge of God's will is through obedience and not sacrifice.

The purpose God has for my life is perfection and each act of obedience confirms it within my heart to be holy in His service. Yes, I have been here before the moment I first believed and certainly will again to please Him.

There will be many days, when I bow myself down in His presence crying out and acknowledging my transgressions *"Purge me with hyssop and I shall be clean"*. *(Psalms 51:7)*. Pressing on towards the mark of this high calling, I entered in, *not my own*, but God's possession, having been fully prepared in righteousness.

The belief in my heart and the desire of my soul is to do God's will and build a kingdom house of faith so I may behold the glory of the Lord and respond. The revelation of my response draws me closer into the center of the eye of omnipotent glory. The voices I heard were singing shouts of "glory, glory, glory."

My lips quivered in agreement and my spirit responded joyfully "glory, glory, glory." A fountain of happiness burst forth from everywhere and no longer was I just a participant in the "act" of participating; I evaporated in spirit-filled worship of the Lord forever!

I found myself being fine-tuned wanting to get closer so I could touch the omniscient love I felt everywhere. God the Father brought me to a place where there is no darkness. He guided me into His "House" where there is only light. Walking in the Spirit I am worthy of such a blessing because His grace and mercy are indestructible.

In my vision, I saw a huge impressive being with glorious wings that made sounds as they moved hinged upon his back like anchors in the deep water. He picked me up with His hands that made waves of light, not the ordinary hands of a man; but hands that made sounds of musical notes I had never heard.

He took me higher and higher up the mountain into spirit and truth by His words, *"Exalt her, and she will promote you; She will bring you honor, when you embrace her"*

(Proverbs 4:8). This place was beyond "up" and no person could ever scale it to the top, the only way up would be to fly. The sides of the mountain seemed like ice crystals and the light around me emitted, yet another musical tone in sequence with the reflection of the lights was revealed as we passed. It was an astounding experience to be so far, "up" that, there is no "down", and I closed my eyes and heard the silence comfort me in an unforgettable blissful moment with the Lord.

It was as if my earthly life was reflecting through the lights and the Spirit of the Lord brought back to me a dream I once had as a child. In this night vision, I saw myself flying but I could only fly above the heads of people who were walking down roads in different directions that I did not.

They were jumping up trying to pull me down into their direction, but they could never make me fall or turn. This was so frustrating to me, I felt like I should be able to go higher and further, but the harder I tried the more they held onto the garments I wore in a feeble attempt to control my movements. No matter what they did, my position never changed and I was still heaven bound, until all they could do was look up at me! This dream was a Joseph prototype where the Spirit of the Lord was showing me things to come. I would one day have rule over the circumstances in my life *that was* meant to destroy me.

I would go places others could not go and no matter how hard they tried to stop me, it would be to no avail. I would one day be in a position where people would have to look up to me whether they wanted to or not. God ordained my life and He covered every possibility of which way I might go to keep me coming back to Him.

My vision was an indicator of a prophetic future to do great works of faith. This work for the Lord would directly affect principalities, powers and people on the earth, represented by the peoples' desire to hold onto my garments.

I would experience a flight to heaven carried in the arms of holiness Himself. It was insight into the life proclaimed by God, as one of righteousness. I humbled myself to be as *low* as I was going high to experience, fully, God's love unlike any words could ever explain. Suddenly my experience was heightening as I felt the softest zephyr caressing my face. It was the feathers of His wings, which had hidden me within them. God was a fortress around me and I am in the secret place of the Highest God! I was in the direct contact with the omnipotent, omniscience, omnipresence of the heart of God!

Spiritually, I had reached the peak of an impact that revealed the glory of who He is. "God is love" and He touched me with His holiness. The Spirit of the Lord said to me, "I am Love and I carry you *to* every place you *go and* have ever been; I then wait for you so that I may return with you; in total esteem; I couldn't speak. My voice silenced, then again my lips trembling softly saying *"glory, glory, glory"* to the "Most High" God forever!

Like apples whose destination is in the hands of the one who plants and then picks them, so was mine in the hands of the Almighty God. He chose me to be His vessel and a witness to believe and trust in His holiness and become like Him. God carries me to and into to my prospective places as a chosen fruit ripened on the vine of love. Throughout the course of my life, the choices I have made landed me at the bottom of barrels of rotting fruit. However, signed, sealed and delivered, He still wrapped me into His likeness to become holy and acceptable in His sight!

It is always the will of God to perfect everything according to His purposes. My position in Him can never change because of my condition. I may face many storms and droughts, but He is my refuge and trust I Him to restore me; I am His. The Lord encourages us according to His plan of salvation and as we obey His command, we have the assurance to have every provision; *"And he shall be like a tree planted by the rivers of water that brings forth his fruit in his season: his leaf also shall not wither; and whatsoever he does shall prosper" (Psalm 1:3).*

The Lord reconciled me through the work of my Lord and Savior Jesus Christ. I have no fear of these close encounters communing with the Lord. "Where are you taking me?" I asked. He replied with longsuffering "I am taking you many places, but you only have one destination, which is to be with me always. I have forever been with you, but you had to grow into who you are now, before you would know."

"Know what my Lord, I asked?" *"Love"*, He replied. *"Jesus said unto him, thou shall love the Lord thy God with all thy heart, and with all thy soul, and with all thy mind. This is the first and great commandment. And the second is like unto it, thou shall love thy neighbor as thyself" (Matthews 22:37-39).* I closed my eyes and prayed "God, thank you for letting me come into the *"Living"* room of your heart; a place alive and filled with your love and eternal kindness forever; a place you've called me to know, which is the great "I AM." Thank you for the privilege to worship and adore you with joy." I will rest in the arms of His love forever by following the perfect model of His Son Jesus Christ.

In the presence of the Most High God and my Lord, my eyes melt into a welcomed comfort and I uttered *"Lord forgive me,* for I, like Eve, I have fallen short of your glory. So much has passed through this vessel, some known and some unknown, but my spirit's desire is to confess them to you now." Moreover, He lifted up His countenance upon me, *"Blessed be the Lord, because He has heard the voice of my supplications! The Lord is my strength and my shield my heart trusted in Him and I am helped. Therefore my heart rejoices greatly, and with my song I will praise Him"* (*Psalms 28: 6-7*). The voice of the Lord is full of majesty He spoke and said, *"Do not be wise in your own eyes; fear the Lord and depart from evil. It will be health to your flesh and strength to your bones. Honor the Lord with all your procession and with the first fruits of all your increase"* (*Proverbs 3:7-9*). Yes, I am *"Eve"* His daughter, as is every woman, who knows that His love covers a multitude of things, and seeks His face for forgiveness.

The Lord is teaching me His ways of blessings and increase; *"He also taught me, and said to me let your heart retain these words; keep my commands and live. Get wisdom! Get understanding! Do not forget, nor turn away from the words of my mouth"* (*Proverbs 4:4-5*). I am captured in the heart of God's everlasting love which He invested in me to teach me to live holy and to greatly understand His wisdom! *Positioned* by God to humility, I cried out "Oh Lord, you are so worthy of all the praise you are Holy and Perfect, *I am yours*." Truly worshipping God, I found this amazing place of total esteem of "who" He is within my heart, which yearns to trust Him.

God purified my heart "the path" that leads to His own heart because I believe in Him…"*I, even I, am He that blotted out thy transgressions for mine own sake, and will not remember thy sins" (Isaiah 43:25).* "*For thus says the high and lofty One that inhabits eternity, whose name is Holy; I dwell in the high and holy place, with Him also that is of a contrite and humble spirit, to revive the spirit of the humble, and to revive the heart of the contrite ones" (Isaiah 57:15).* God is awesome and it is a privilege to experience His love, because He says, "*I love them that love me; and those that seek me early shall find me" (Proverbs 8:17).*

God's heart is the place where all matters of those who receive Him are settled. Trembling I looked into the light that was holding me and closely guarding me. I know I have the protection of the Lord because *"He that dwelleth in the secret place of the most high shall abide under the shadow of the Almighty. I will say of the Lord, He is my refuge and my fortress; my God; in Him will I trust. Surely, He shall deliver thee from the snare of the fowler, and from the noisome pestilence. He shall cover thee under His feathers, and under His wings shall thou trust; His truth shall be your shield and buckler. Thou shall not be afraid for the terror by night; nor for the arrow that flies by day. Nor for the pestilence that walks in the darkness; nor for the destruction that waste at noonday. A thousand shall fall at thy side, and ten thousand at thy right hand; but it shall not come neigh thee. Only with thine eyes, shall thou behold and see the reward of the wicked. Because thou have made the Lord, which is my refuge, even the most High, thy habitation; there shall no evil befall thee neither shall any plague come near thy dwelling. For He shall give His angels charge over thee, to keep thee in all thy ways. They shall bear thee up in their hands, lest thou dash thy foot against a stone. Thou shall tread upon the lion and the adder; the young lion and the dragon shall thou trample under feet. Because He has set His love upon me, therefore will I deliver him: I will set him on high, because he has known my name. He shall call upon me, and I will answer him: I will be with him in trouble; I will deliver him and honor him. With long life will I satisfy him, and show him my salvation" (Psalm 91).*

My love for the Lord expresses itself in these words... "Lying in the perpetual loom of the imminent breaking of day, I am blooming into the light. The light warms my cold hands, I reached up to touch the face of love, and it stood still." Moreover, love said, "I have been waiting for you to touch me, for I am all that you have never been without. I am the watch tower you look for in the storm, I am He that you seek, and I am love who awakens love."

I found the gate to the heart of God, for He is love. Now that I am there, I want to recline in the soft goodness of His mercy forever. I love God, and I want to be in His presence, I want to talk to Him and share myself with Him as He has given us His all!" The Lord teaches me to number my days so that I may gain a heart of wisdom! According to Genesis 1:1-6, the darkness of the fall had to be lifted and a flicker of light showed a future of hope.

Eve's name reflected the remarkable role she would have to play in the history of man, and as for the faith, Adam had to speak it; for there had not been any births and He said, *"Your name shall be called Eve, the mother of all living things" (Genesis 3:20).*

Eve realized that she, the guilty sinner, could serve her gracious and forgiving God. Her name spoke a promise and indicated that by bearing Adam's children she would become the mother of all generations. Eve, thankful to God's mercy, learned to totally trust in His Word alone.

Eve, from a downfall she still birthed life; from darkness came light; from an end, a new beginning; from the curse, a blessing; from her sentence to death, a hope for the future; from the vicious anguish of defeat, to the strength of a promising faith; Eve was the mother of all living things. This remarkable epic of humanity gives us hope just as it did Adam and Eve. My life is significant to God enough to give me deep roots in Him. The Lord gave

Eve the hope of restoration to pass on, and I have it also; I have faith. I choose to sit at the feet of the Lord giving up my presence to find His with the expectation of a greater work to come.

Eve was the hallmark of God's creative work. She was the first of Adam's race; the last living thing to be called into existence. She was actually crafted by the Almighty hands of God. God made Adam of refined dirt; Eve was the glorious crown of the human race and a very special gift to Adam to make his existence whole.

Eve was the first ever woman of God, the first ever wife, and the first answer to Adam's incompleteness. She complemented Adam and was his helper; a position of honor, *"the glory of man" (I Corinthians 11:7).*

The light of God's love magnified within me to understand that Eve's" forgiveness was as all of humanity redeemed by the Lord Jesus Christ. In humbleness, all wickedness wanes for priority over my freewill choice to choose the Lord's decree. Rhema Revelations are the light whose brilliance boost the evening into my day, to know joy comes in the morning if I choose God. My process of sanc-tification strengthens me and gives me the confidence to know my relationship with the Lord can never be broken again; this I can be confident.

My confession came from the deepest part of eternity within me and I wanted to let it all go, everything that I knew. I wanted it to be over so I could rest in His arms forever and so I cried out, "I am a sinner and I repent in the Name of Jesus Christ and ask for forgiveness.

I know God heard me and that I am received of the beloved and I am so godly sorrowed, but I rejoiced because the voice of the Lord is mightier than the roaring waters. *"If we confess our sins, He is faithful and just to forgive us our sins, and to cleanse us from all unrighteousness" (1 John 1:9).*

"Daughter, do you know why you have come back to me?" My spirit whispered meekly "Yes Lord, I belong to you and your love beckoned my return, I'm here to ask you great things that I have forgotten and to see you in your fullness.

21

I had been living conditionally in the flesh, without the perfected knowledge of walking worthy in the Spirit of the Living God. I am weak and I need your strength to learn fully to seek you Lord God, *"Not by might, nor by power, but by my Spirit, said the Lord of Hosts" (Zechariah 4:6).*

My lips pierced with salvation, and I continued to lay silently still in the arms of vindication. I wanted to be like Him and my life transformed into one of holiness; my desires became all things that was good, perfect, lovely and of a good report.

I felt as if I was visiting a close friend's house and was welcomed in every room, so I went into their most private place; the closet. Now, I knew the clothes they wore and in my admiration of them, I wanted to wear the same garments as they did. I tried on the garments of righteousness and I can fit them, and still others, *(the other garments in the closet),* I need to mature into spiritually.

This is how it feels to go deeply into the heart of God learning what He wears. All the clothes are royal garments and they must be custom fitted by God's holiness and righteousness to His vessels. *"Let the priests be clothed with righteousness; and let thy saints shout for joy"(Psalm 132:9).*

Glory to the Lord! Now it seems that I must come from the closet, but not until I hear Him call my name. Finally, as I draw nearer to him it happens "Daughter, are you hiding from me again?"

"And they heard the sound of the Lord God walking in the garden in the cool of the day, and Adam and his wife Eve hid themselves from the presence of the Lord God among the trees of the garden. Then the Lord God called to Adam and said to him, "Where are you?" So he said, "I heard your voice in the garden and I was afraid because I was naked and I hid myself" and He said, "who told you that you were naked? Have you eaten from the tree of which I commanded you that you should not eat? Then the man said, "The woman you gave to be with me, she gave me of the tree and I ate." And the Lord God said to the women, what is this you have done?" (Genesis 3:8-13). The blood of the Lamb has redeemed me and I am no longer ashamed, hidden away

from God's love. It is evident the shame of Adam and Eve was coupled with fear and reproof; that is why they tried to hide their inadequacy with fig leaves.

Nothing could cover the shame and the horror of telling God what they had done. They never confessed fully, but I can and I do; *"Forgive me Oh God."* All attempts of humanity to hide from God are always inadequate, for God is all knowing and forever present. It was man who had forgotten Him, not Him who forgot about man.

In Genesis 3:14-19 is the Lord's response to the action of His children and the serpent; so the Lord said to the serpent, *"Because you have done this, you are cursed more than all cattle, and more than every beast of the field; on your belly you shall go, and you shall eat dust all the days of your life. And I will put enmity between you and the woman and between your seed and her seed. He shall bruise your head, and you shall bruise his heel,"* to the woman He said, *"I will greatly multiply your sorrow and your conception; in pain you shall bring forth children; your desire shall be for your husband, and he shall rule over you."* Then to Adam

He said, "Because you have heeded the voice of your wife, and have eaten from the tree of which I commanded you, saying, "You shall not eat of it" cursed is the ground for your sake; in toil you shall eat of it all the days of your life. Both thorns and thistles it shall bring forth for you, and you shall eat the herb of the field. In the sweat of your face you shall eat bread till you return to the ground, for out of it you were taken; for dust you are, and to dust you shall return."

Thus, the fall of the human race. However, God did not forget about *us* and did not *condemn* Adam and Eve to carry the burden of sin forever. If we fail and even if our enemies beguiled us, we still have hope, *"But we have this treasure in earthen vessels that the Excellency of the power may be of God, and not of us. We are troubled on ever side, yet not distressed; we are perplexed, but not in despair, per-secuted, but not forsaken; cast down, but not destroyed" (II Corinthians 4:7-9).*

The burden of mistake and failure is much too heavy for us to carry for we all have sinned and fallen short of the glory of the Lord according to Romans 3:23. That is why God's curse upon humanity included the mercy and grace of hope, God expressed His love for Adam and Eve because they lived to be the parents of the world.

He could have simply destroyed them, but God is merciful and full of grace. Thank God that in spite of our problems we can maintain hope. A declaration of our hope builds our faith in the providence of the Lord. The Word of God tells us *"I have written your name on my hand" (Isaiah 49:16);* and I am always with God. I want Him to have total possession of the glory of my existence; and I must surrender.

It is all for God's namesake that I have been invited to the most wanted place in eternity, to stand in the presence of God before Him in love and not be guilty or ashamed. This is my private spa of forgiveness and love pouring out the oil of my salvation upon my soul with peace.

The mouth of God opens for me as He whispers kindness through the breath of His love in His holiness. My heart knows His voice and fills with anticipation for the work ahead; I surrender to the will of the Lord. His concern for me is my greatest assurance in His Word for me to *"Trust in the Lord with all thine heart; and lean not unto your own understanding. In all thy ways acknowledge Him, and He shall direct your path" (Proverbs 3:5-6).*

The Spirit of the Lord wraps me in the lap of joy and hides me in the hollows of His hands, and I am fulfilled, forever satisfied in Him. God designed a plan for me; I have been requested before the foundation of the world into a milieu where everything was and is to come. I may not see it, feel it or know it logically, but by faith it is there, yes my Lord is there.

The invitation is open to bring my thirst to receive living water by the Creator Himself; my RSVP is faith. *"I can bring my hunger and I will be given bread of life. I come naked and I am clothed."* It is God who has called me, *"Come unto me all ye that labor and are heavy laden, and I will give you rest" (Matthews 11:28).*

God is moved by compassion and I trust Him to comfort me in my darkness. He will bring me to His closet and fill me with His light if I let Him in. *"Why art thou cast down, O my soul and why art thou disquieted within me? Hope thou in God" (Psalm 42:11).*

I stand in the stillness of love and I hear footsteps beyond the door I have entered. I heard a small knock and I perceived someone leaning close to the door listening for my response. They knocked again and a weak "who is it" comes up from my spirit.

If I draw near to God then He will draw near to me, *"For the Son of man come not to be ministered unto, but to minister, and give His life as a ransom for many" (Matthew 20:28).*

"May I come in?" the Spirit of the Lord asked, I looked down at myself and I was naked spiritually. I had to make up my mind to let God in as I was. There was no place to go and I finally decided I could not hide from God in His own closet; He brought me here to teach me who He was.

I surrendered and the lights came on within me, for there is no darkness in my Lord, and He dwells within me. Now I could see the closet is my own, and the beautiful garments God wants me to wear are predestined; and as I grow in Him, they will fit me well. I have great expectations to wear the clothes of holiness, righteousness, garments of praise and a holy crown. Exposing my flesh crucifies it, the anointing of God destroys its yoke, and His goodness cloaks me.

I had made a decision not to be like Adam and Eve; that is to not hide from God; nor blame others for my shortcomings, and be blessed by accepting and confessing them! They were inadequate, hiding and trembling with guilt; lacking the understanding of the love before them, and yet another first as they stood in the presence of the Lord ashamed and filled with fear.

Adam and Eve's experience leaves me a valuable lesson, which is to love God above all things and never be afraid to repent of falling short of His glory! The Almighty hand of God was knocking on their hearts to repent yet they did not. Fearful, they refused to look back into the heart of God as their Father. God yearned to show them His love is unfailing and if they trusted Him, He would have guided them back to righteousness. No weapon formed against me shall prosper, especially one set from my own hands, I said "Yes and Amen Lord!"

My repentance gives me a way out of no way to stand holy and righteous in the heart of God. The choice is always mine to accept God's offer of royal clothes *(the blood of Jesus)* to wear to cover my shame and guilt. I came out of the fear so I could walk in obedience perfecting the strength of God within my weakness, and believing *"He is the one who called me out of darkness into His marvelous light" (I Peter 2:9).*

It was nothing else I had to do but say "yes" and Jehovah Jireh did the rest: *"Therefore my heart is glad, and my glory rejoices: my flesh shall also rest in hope" (Psalms 16:9).* I am so grateful to the Lord because I was once a lonely, worldly straggler, stumbling in the darkness, wondering what to do; weak and uncertain of my steps, I said "yes" to the soft knock of the heart of God in my life.

I am not an orphan any longer, I belong to God who sees me in my nakedness and still loves me. He personally fitted me in mercy with His garments of holiness and righteousness by His Word. God called my name, He was waiting to see my face turn to Him, I was the one God was seeking to wear His garments of praise.

He is my Father; my Creator; the loving Shepherd who found me lost and saved me through His Son; my Lord Jesus Christ. I was the wandering stray sheep waiting to hear His gentle voice afraid and in need.

"Oh, how long I've awaited thee Oh God, and I am "EVE" on the dawn of a new day; the mother of all living things full of hope." Finally, arriving in the fullness of the Lord within my soul, and as Eve desired to reproduce a seed of life that God would be pleased, I want to please God with fruitfulness as well.

The Spirit of God said that I would gain a greater understanding of who I am in the plan of an Almighty God. I have been reborn in the image of the only begotten Son of God, a new creature capable of great and mighty things because I am His workmanship. God has His hands on me; I am a "Woman of God" who shall rise with life in her belly by trusting the Lord. I have the hope that was formed from the foundation of the world and all the things God has promised to add to...I am God's daughter!

My desire is to *"first seek the Kingdom of God and His righteousness, then He will add these things"* (Matthew *6:33).* The Holy Spirit is teaching me to hold on to His unchanging hand and to face every challenge guided in holiness.

All for the glory and victory of the Kingdom of God, I yield in the Name of Jesus. I am like "Eve" who have walked from the sleeping Adam, formed from His rib (Genesis 2:21-25), into humanity, to show the grace of the Lord through the mistakes she made and those we will all make.

Adam and Eve fell short of the glory of God; but they came back strong through their offspring whom God promised, His name is Jesus. Thank You, Lord for you have given the world a man who came out of the body of a woman not touched by the blood of sin. "Eve" and "Adam" the forgiven parents of the human race, a wonderful demonstration of God's love, grace, and mercy, and prefect wisdom of His plan of salvation. I am here to bear witness to truth of obedience and unity of faith by developing a heart for righteousness and a soul for holiness; I am the redeemed of the Lord!

I have found Holy ground to stand upon and say I am like Eve (helper to others) made to fill the void of Adam (the human race), I'm his helper and so shall it be (1 Corinthians 11:8-9). I will walk again in the joy of the true paradise of God's design in full participation of His creation. All sin is already been forgiven by God's provisional plan to save humanity from the Garden of Eden to this very moment.

We are no longer at the gate wanting to come in; we are indeed in the full participation of it. The Lord's words of hope and a promise of freedom before the origin of the world refreshes us, *"He came and sent a crushing blow to the head of the enemy," and* this is "The first Gospel" (Genesis 3:15) and there is no fear. This was good news for the fallen state of man; Jesus Christ, who was uniquely

"Born of a woman" (Galatians 4:4) came and paid the full transaction for us all! The offspring of a virgin, God in human form, and literally fulfilled the promise of God, that the seed of the woman would bruise the serpent's head.

Eve, the hopeful one who found God's kindness, compassion and forgiveness resting in her seed to save the world. All her children are tokens of joyful prayers to the Lord. She knew somewhere in her linage one would turn the Father's eyes back upon them in pleasure. Honoring His goodness is a reminder of His authority she laid hope in her heart designed for the justification of humanity to come forth.

The blood is no longer on her hands but on the cross and her redemption came through her offspring Jesus Christ. A Godly line has endured in the faith of the Lord since that day, and joy came into the world again as the legacy of life and defeated death forever. Rejoice in the celebration of the work of the Redeemer; the work of the Lord Jesus Christ, the only begotten Son of the Father.

Come out of the closet of darkness and walk as a light of the world; wear the clothes of holiness, righteousness, and garments of praise from the Lord.

God has provided covering for our nakedness from the beginning, why are you hiding in your flesh? It's over! We are the redeemed of the Lord! Come out from among them that do not believe and walk in the Spirit with your Lord and worship the Lord! Worship is our act of attributing honor, reverence, or worth to the Lord, which acknowledges His sovereign authority of power over all things.

It magnifies Him in honor as the Triune God, God the Father, God the Son and God the Holy Spirit. When we worship the Lord, "we are" is in response to the self-revelation of our powerlessness in the hands of the Almighty God.

God divinely reveals himself, His purposes and His will to us through Jesus Christ; we then develop a spiritual and personal relationship with God as a worshipper. Experiencing the initiation of God's Spirit, we respond in adoration, humility, submission, and obedience to God. It becomes a way of life, totally giving one's self to the Lord and trusting His purpose *"I beseech you therefore brethren, by the mercies of God that ye present your bodies a living sacrifice, holy and acceptable unto God, which is our reasonable service" (Romans 12:1).* Jesus is a perfect example of this total submission.

The Bible says, *"And He went a little farther, and fell on His face and prayed, saying, O Father, if it be possible, let this cup pass me: nevertheless not as I will, but as thou wilt" (Matthew 26:39).*

LESSON

We must wait on the Lord by faith and trusting Him for our well being totally handing over His creation back into His hands with great expectations as Jesus proved. How many times have we sought God in our hearts and never thought to turn and enter into His? The revelation of the heart of God towards us builds trust and faith that becomes alive and vibrant, growing into the knowledge of the Living God.

We become rooted and grounded and in agreement with God's desires for us to be righteous and holy. In all that I have experienced on this journey, whoever I thought I was before the arms of God's wisdom, understanding and knowledge picked me up, I was not that person anymore. I am a new creature bonded to Him alone.

I am the righteousness of God's faithfulness, God's promise, God's goodness and I am blessed (Deuteronomy 28:2-12). I am a "woman" of God personally created in His image to mirror back the reflection of His glory.

Every time I reach out in love, perform a deed of kindness, soften my heart in forgiveness, show a little extra patience and follow through in faithfulness, I am reflecting the character of God. As a worshipper honoring His will, I seek a deeper relationship with the Lord in meekness.

I resolve to walk by faith and not by sight; in thanksgiving and praise rejoicing in the precious promises of the glory of the Lord. He is Faithful and I am more than an ordinary participant; I am in the full participation of God's perfect will, holy and acceptable in His sight.

The Spirit of the Lord has shown me all these things.

Amen!

II

YES

YES

YES

Despite the troubled beginning of humanity, we are justified by the presence of the promises of the Father. He gave us everything we needed in His Word as an incorruptible seed, *"In the beginning was the Word, and the Word was with God and the Word was God" (John 1:1).*

The mighty voice of God provides us with a plan of salvation; our hope for a future. God, the Creator, spoke the heavens; the earth; the mountains and the valleys into existence. The mountains and valleys reflect to us a similitude of the highs and lows of our lives.

Our high times provide us with the joy of trusting and believing God who gave us a way out of all our difficulties. During those times when there seems to be nothing before us, we can still have that joy and confidence. God restores us through the work of His Son Jesus Christ; and even in the midst of despair, there is hope. God's proclaimed Word, His holiness and His sovereign authority all have the power to transform all things.

The low times are good times because God teaches us about the aspects of our personal character that opposes Him. The low times helps us to recognize the need to run out of self- willed options, resources and ideas. At this point, we should realize there is no reprieve and come before God with a broken and contrite heart.

With our willingness to become empty of ourselves, God's perfect will then saves us. He is the Lord of the mountains and the valleys and we must trust and believe in Him for all things. He will never, never, never leave or forsake us! There is great expectation resting in our faith by trusting in the Lord; imagine living without the hope of finding a way out of the lows in life.

There once was a man who experienced this phenomenon of a life without hope and doomed by circumstances. The man was a living and breathing person rejected by others as if he were dead; even though he was alive, he had not lived. He was a diseased leper who wore dirty rags to cover the shame of his withering body; he was avoided, an outcast, untouchable and unloved.

His face masked with scraps of cloth hiding the visage of death and not allowed to live within the city. However, for the very necessities of his living daily, he had to return, which was never an easy task.

The closer he came he was required to carry a bell clanking it noisily while crying out in a loud voice, warning others of his soon arrival. The people who dwelled within the city were thereby alerted of his approach and the words "UNCLEAN, UNCLEAN" resounded, and the path before him was cleared. He hopelessly fulfilled a sentence of death and accepted the heartbreak of his despair; ejected and abandoned he steadily cried out "UNCLEAN, UNCLEAN."

People avoided him like the plague, there were never words of comfort spoken to him; he was a dead man walking, who needed only a burial. He was a feared man not because he was evil, but because others feared contracting the disease; they would not even look at him and literally turned their backs on him. Rejection and fear tormented him daily.

He must have been quite grieved not only mentally, but also physically, spiritually and socially thinking, "I'm alone." The disease had eaten away at his body; and the loneliness devoured away at his heart. No one ever reached out to help him and so it seemed he was utterly alone; but not without hope.

He had recently heard about a man who was a healer and was on a mission to find Him. He entered into the city at the risk of death to find life; for the first time he was not afraid because he had found hope. Jesus was the man he had heard about that was so powerful He could even make a leper clean again.

He soon found Jesus and humbled himself kneeling at His feet; he looked up with watering eyes and pleaded to the only man who ever looked into them, he cried "if you are willing, you could make me clean." Jesus moved by compassion and love knew the anticipation of His heart.

He reached out touched him and said "I am willing", and the leper was healed. It took much courage for the leper to offer himself openly, knowing no one had ever tried to help him, but he trusted Jesus and he was cleansed.

Jesus is the "Man of Sorrows" who knows the hurt and pain of suffering and His love purified him. What was inside of this man was the faith that God gives every one of His children.

It is a ticket, which divides the light from the darkness; God takes pleasure in seeing us *"hold on"* to it and *"believe"* in it. God's precious promises are folded neatly into our souls and when we worship and trust Him, they expand. Jesus is the lover of our soul and He will never turn us away. He receives us even when we are seemly unacceptable.

Jesus will heal us and make us holy and acceptable in His sight..."*Who shall separate us from the love of Christ? Shall tribulation, or distress, or persecution, or famine, or nakedness, or peril, or sword? As it is written, for thy sake we are killed all the daylong; we are accounted as sheep for the slaughter. Nay, in all these things we are more than conquerors through him that loved us. For I am persuaded, that neither death, nor life, nor angles, nor principalities, nor powers, nor things present, not things to come, nor height, nor depth, nor any other creature, shall be able to separate us from the love of God, which is in Christ Jesus our Lord"* *(Romans 8:35-39).*

LESSON

The leper's faith and the compassionate love of God is what restored him and made him whole. God does the same for all who are willing to take the opportunity to trust Him. God is the Creator of all things. When we look up into the heavens, we see the mighty works of God.

The stars are His creative works, suspended only by Him, the curtain that pulls down the darkness with the light, only He could do that. What will we ever experience in life that disturbs our peace and twists our emotions that God cannot fix? Nothing!

God is Almighty and has sovereign power over His creation; He unseals the sun light and places His children above the darkness! God does these wonders for us because He is God and has the power to change anything. Nothing is impossible for Him! *"And the earth was without form, and void; and darkness was upon the face of the deep. And the Spirit of God moved upon the face of the waters. And God said let there be light. And God saw the light, that it was good: and God divided the light from the darkness"* *(Genesis 1:3-4)*.

The leper was healed of a "dark" disease into the "light" of total transformation, all for the glory of the Lord. God will not leave us in the darkness. We praise God, *"Now unto Him that is able to do exceedingly and abundantly above all that we ask, or think, according to the power that works in us"(Ephesians 3:20)*. God's love has provided us with all that we need, and if we trust and believe in His love and obey Him, we will be cleansed of all darkness!

III

LOOK INSIDE FIRST

God placed within us, the power to glorify Him; He has never left any one of His chosen, nor has He forsaken them. The power we need is the power we already have. If we search long enough without becoming wearied there is nothing we cannot achieve. God has not forgotten anything concerning us, *"I can do all things through Christ which strengthens me" (Philippians 4:13).*

Recall the classic story of Dorothy in the Wizard of Oz; we all know how it feels to find ourselves in places where we don't belong. Our paths might not be the yellow brick road Dorothy experienced and hopefully the path we are on will ultimately lead us back to a place of comfort and joy.

We may also find similarities in the witches we run into along this route and learn they want more than our ruby slippers; they want our souls. Dorothy is not the only person to have lost their way, or find out the people around them are like the Scarecrow who was without wisdom and sometimes unthinking; some will be heartless like the Tin Man; others without courage like the cowardly Lion.

Each of her friends seemly lacked a necessary component needed to accomplish great tasks. We can relate to Dorothy's paradox. After facing many challenges, Dorothy enters into Emerald City, the Land of Oz, and meets the Wizard whose great powers could grant them their wishes. Trembling with fear, they one by one stood before him and made their requests known, he responded with an imposing thunderous voice.

He told them that he would help, but they had to demonstrate their worthiness. They had to overcome the wicked witch who worked evilness in the Land of Oz. "Bring me back the witch's broom" he told them and then "I'll help you." They went and accomplished what he asked, they scaled the castle walls where she lived and made wax of the witch destroying her evil powers. In the process, they make some startling discoveries of the hidden things within and around them. They discovered they could overcome evil without the power of the "so called" Wizard, who later was exposed to be an ordinary man with his own dreams and fears.

The drama ends with Dorothy discovering that her worst nightmare was in reality, just a bad dream, and also that her "somewhere over the rainbow" home was right where she had always been and that the people around her, yet imperfect, was all she had. She realized that it is nice to have friends in high places; some of which you can believe in and some you cannot. She discovered that she had the power all the time to go back home within her, but she had to believe it first.

The moral of the Wizard of Oz is the fact that an all-powerful God has placed everything we need inside of us and if we believe, we can get back home to where He is. The prerequisites are that it happens only after we learn to appreciate where He positions us to begin the journey. The power to overcome is inside of our hearts, and if we stop looking outside our self, we will find contentment wherever

God has placed us. Trusting only in Gods' desires reflects our renewed mind's wisdom to be His without fear, knowing *"But my God shall supply all your needs according to His riches in glory by Christ Jesus" (Philippians 4:19).*

The world tells us if we try hard enough, we can make ourselves into passionate, powerful and purposeful human beings, all we need is to bridle our own potential. This vote of self- righteousness causes delays and setbacks in our service to God.

We can do nothing successfully without surrendering it first to God. The Word of God stands against such a mindset and empowers us to have a renewed mind *"Not by might, nor by power, but by my Spirit, said the Lord of Hosts" (Zechariah 4:6).*

TESTIMONY

Without the power of the Holy Spirit working inside of me, I would still be trapped in the world doing all the terrible things the world does. I would still believe I had power to change the circumstances of my life not recognizing that it was God keeping me alive. I should have been dead, but I survived the ugliness of being in the streets practicing all kinds of immorality; simply because God is the Master over my life and not me. I would still be wasting precious opportunities to say "Thank You Lord" living a depraved existence, ignorant of Him!

I am grateful for the desperation God allowed to over-take me, to stop me, to heal me, to want Him as much as He wanted me. He is the Mighty Endless "One God" who gave me one more day every day until I said, "yes Lord", until I became perfected (matured), until I knew His voice and refused to followed another.

He loved me, protected me and made me a holy wom-an of God for His glory! The Holy Spirit directed me out of the agony of the flesh which I've termed the *"Trinity Of Death,"* me, myself and I, to make a decision not to be left behind in the darkness. I decree and declare that I am a chosen instrument of the "Most High" God!

He has engaged in me a desire to live in Him. I am bound by faith to help others find that same road to devel-op a sense of contentment, a renewed mind, divine boldness, a pure heart and the courage to live righteous and holy! The power is within me to do all things through Christ by trusting Him at His word. He will help me through the difficult times. He completes the "BIG" picture of my life story. I await Him in the most intimate places of who I am; He comes to me as close as I come to Him.

I am humbled, bringing God what I thought was the whole me, just to find out they were mere pieces of *"who am I supposed to be in Him."* The greatest treasure I have found in my life is that I am a temple of God and that it is in Him that I live, move and have my being (Acts 17:28). What a revelation and discovery to have once lived as a child of disobedience believing I was just a "nobody."

I am rejoicing that I am a temple for God, holy and acceptable in His sight! My life changed as the Holy Spirit taught me who I am in Christ and that I belonged to Him. My willingness to grow in that knowledge as God's child is paramount and not negotiable. Upon this foundation, I am victorious. As I emptied my life into God's hands, I received three miracles: "Restoration, Recovery and Renewal." In this ongoing perfection (maturation), what remains is "spiritual cleanliness" and the wisdom to live it as a daily reprieve.

Oh praise God, for He is so good and the Holy Spirit of God is within me; He makes me glad... *"Nevertheless I tell you the truth; it is expedient for you that I go away; for if I go not away, the Comforter will not come unto you; but if I depart, I will send Him unto you. And when He is come, He will reprove the world of sin, and of righteousness, because I go to my Father, and ye see me no more; of judgment, because the prince of this world is judged. I have yet many things to say unto you, but ye cannot bear them now. Howbeit when He the Spirit of Truth, is come, He will guide you into all truth: for He shall not speak of himself; but whatsoever He shall hear, that shall He speak: and He will show you things to come. He shall glorify me; for He shall receive of mine, and shall show it unto you"* (John 16:7-14). The man of truth and loyal promises is always with me Jesus said, *"I will ask the Father, and He will give you another*

Helper to be with you forever, the Spirit of Truth. The world cannot accept Him. But you know, because He lives with you and will be in you" (John 14:16-17).

PRAYER

Oh, thank you Lord for I am worthy to be a partaker of your glory because you called me and I have answered. I am brought to my knees to worship you Lord with thanksgiving in my heart and I give you all of the honor and praise. The Gift of the Holy Spirit is holiness, which lives in me as a tangible expression of the loving care and tender mercies of Jesus Christ.

I know that no matter what I have done in the past, He perfected every breech of all flesh and I have peace because the battle is already won. I am fixed because Jesus paid it all for me to know that "God is Love."

I waited for years in a state of deprivation and turmoil for someone to look into my eyes and see the "leper" reaching out for help." It never happened until I found Jesus was my life and the treasure of truth and holiness existed inside of me. What seems simple now was quite

53

difficult before I found that my answers were never in the substances other than faith that I picked up to ease the pain; they had appeared as angels of light to consume me.

They were on a mission to steal my purpose of living to ensure that my faith in my Lord and Savior Jesus Christ, would never surface. The promises of God are true; even during the darkest periods when it seems like God had abandoned His plans concerning me, something happened.

The promises always came through when things were getting worse in my life, the voice of God called me and I turned around. Each time I heard Him whisper my name. I knew...He is not finished with me yet and that He has more hidden treasures laid up for me.

Being a new creature is an ongoing and eternal attribute of my inheritance. Each *moment* I learn to live holy and righteous, I become more and more like Him.

I am confident I belong to Him, *"And the sheep listen to the voice of the shepherd. He calls His own sheep by name and leads them out" (John 10:3) "Here I am I stand at the door and knock. If anyone hears my voice and opens the door I will come in and sup with Him, and he with me"* *(Revelation 3:20). Amen!*

LESSON

The world beats on the door of my life; my Lord Jesus simply taps at the door of my heart. The voices of the world scream for my allegiance, the voice of the Lord Jesus is a soft and tender request to humble my heart and to be His. The promises of the world are temporary pleasures of the flesh and certain death.

Jesus' promises are eternal and I can stay in His presence forever. Imagine looking in the face of God our sweet Savior, understanding that the "glory" is in saying "Holy, Holy, Holy" without ever having to blink...there is no darkness in Him! *I understand so much more now than I first began this journey!*

IV

THE WORLD CAN NEVER HAVE ME AGAIN!

"Ye are of God, little children and have overcome them; because greater is He that is in me then him that is in the world" (1 John 4:4).

My mother introduced me to the Bible and her favorite scripture the 23rd Psalm, which has guided me throughout my life as the first revelation of whose I am. Because it was so dear to my mother and the only part of the Bible that she knew to teach her children, she helped me to memorize it, but not until over forty years later am I studying it to see it in detail; this is such a great awakening for me.

I thought I had received all I could from this familiar passage, but my relationship with the Lord has taken me to a completely new level with greater clarity of being a child of God. Most everyone knows the 23rd Psalm by heart and it has ministered to our deepest needs learning to mature through its percepts. David's walk with God was written during a time when his own son rebelled against him and took the throne.

David's life was in danger and he was forced to flee into the Judean wilderness; the same place he was in where he spent much time as a young shepherd, and for a while could not reclaim his throne. David's circumstances brought him to the very edge of the Shepherd's Seat Experience as he recalls the days past.

This Psalm addresses those, who like David, feel and become uprooted in their life, shaken and in turmoil, seek to find strength in the midst of the wilderness; he cries out *"The Lord is my Shepherd and I shall not want, He makes me to lie down in green pasture, He leads me beside the still waters. He restores my soul; He leads me down a path of righteousness for His namesake. Yea through I walk through the valley of the shadow of death I will fear no evil; for thou art with me; thy rod and thy staff they comfort me. Thou prepares a table before me in the presence of mine enemies; thou anoints my head with oil; my cup runs over surely goodness and mercy shall follow me all the days of my life and I will dwell in the house of the Lord forever"* *(Psalms 23).*

David begins *"The Lord is my Shepherd, I shall not want"* and his soul agrees because God had gathered him into a secret place to protect him from the enemy. He pleads his circumstance to the "Most High" God who heard his cries and sought him to give him what he needed. Like David, I do not lack anything and every need has been satisfied when I follow God.

If there is emptiness and loneliness in my life, I have not allowed the Lord to be my Shepherd, which is a primary requirement for sanctification of the Shepherd's Seat Experience. This anointing is a superabundance of all hope and glory that only God can satisfy the thirst within my soul.

I belong to the Lord, a sheep of His pasture, delivered out of the mouths of ravenous wolves by grace. Many times, we allow ourselves to be shepherded by emotions becoming hopeless, and without out a Savior we are lost in the wilderness. This is when we become discouraged, facing certain death on a path of unrighteousness; we should know that *"The Good Shepherd will never lead me astray.*

By ourselves *"We are like sheep who have gone astray; we have turned everyone to his own way" (Isaiah 53:6).* Leading a life of self-indulgent individualism, doing one's own thing, we are liken to sheep, who without a shepherd suffer greatly. They do not even know when to come out of the storm without that guidance.

David said, *"He makes me to lie down in green pastures" (23:2).* A point to consider is that we do not realize our feebleness. We have to be made to surrender our lives to receive our blessings. The flesh is weak and reckless and a lifestyle outside of the will of the Lord is death.

We must learn that lifestyles leading us away from God must always be rejected and not allowed into our environment. In the analogy of the sheep, I would have rather been an elephant strong and mighty; but it turns out that I am a weak and feeble sheep in human clothing. Sheep are not very smart animals, they are dumb, they are dirty, very meek and in need of every need being provided for them. They depend strictly on the shepherd because they are defenseless; they are in dire need of protection and provision.

We are the sheep of God's pasture. We fit this pattern and are in constant need of a Shepherd. Without the guidance of the Holy Spirit we are subject to our outer man's self-destructive traits; we will wander endlessly lacking wisdom and strength to stand still!

We need Jesus Christ to lead us beside the still waters (23:3). Sheep are fearful of the sound that running water makes, and will only drink from a quiet pool. They would certainly die of thirst without a Good Shepherd who knows just where to take them. They are at peace because the shepherd has met their needs.

Here we can see the provisions of God who feeds the sheep in green pastures (23:2). Now He gives them water for their thirst (23:3). God restores our inner man through His Word as a Shepherd who feeds and waters His flock with loving care. Take heed dear sheep and *"Do not labor for the food which perishes, but for the food which endures to eternal life, which the Son of man will give to you; for on Him has God the Father set His seal."*

Then they said to Him, 'What must we do to be doing the works of God?" Jesus answered them, "This is the work of God, that you believe in Him who He has sent." So they said to Him, "Then what signs do you do, that we may see, and believe you? What work do you perform? Our Father ate manna in the wilderness; as it is written, "He gave them bread from heaven to eat."

Jesus said to them, "Truly, truly, I say to you, it was not Moses who gave you the bread from heaven; my Father gives you the true bread from heaven. "For the bread of God is that which comes down from heaven and gives life to the world" they said to Him, "Lord, give us this bread always." Jesus said to them "I am the bread of life; He who comes to me shall not hunger, and He who believes in me shall never thirst" (John 6:27-35). The Lord restores us as we by faith get to know Him and act upon His Word. Saints, everything that we need is found in our Shepherd...in the person of Christ. God is our only resource and our souls can only be nourished by Him. The Good Shepherd gives us direction in life, *"He leads me in paths of righteousness for His name sake (23:3)."*

The sheep would never make it without their shepherd, because even when the path to follow is obvious they cannot find their way. They are still prone to wander away and become so lost that they cannot find their own way home. Have you ever felt lost, not know what to do, and was embarrassed by the fact you were saved and still sometimes felt lost? It is a normal behavioral characteristic of a sheep to be lost and indecisive; and they need the guidance of a shepherd!

To God is all the glory due, because He knows where we are even when we do not know. There is an ageless story that speaks to the feeling of being lost about a young man in basic training. He was on "KP" duty to sort potatoes, and before him was a huge mound of them; his job was to put all the bad potatoes in the green barrel and all the good potatoes in the orange bucket. The Sergeant in charge came to check on his progress and saw the man holding one potato just staring at it. He noticed there was nothing in either the green barrel or the orange bucket and the sergeant asked, "Is the work too hard?" The solider said, "It's not the work; it's the decisions that are hindering me."

What a typical point of view of a lost sheep, and left to our own devices we will not accomplish the simplest task without the direction of the Holy Spirit! God's will for us is the key to all enlightenment, which is to follow the leader by living a surrendered life with the Lord Jesus Christ as our Shepherd.

Another key is we to admit we are lost and do not know the way to get home, we will never find the way on our own. Jesus said, *"If the eye is single, then the whole body will be full of light. If the eye is dual (or evil), how great is that darkness" (Luke 11:34).*

Focusing on the Lord Jesus, our lives will be filled with His light, which is the Way, the Truth and the Life; and the only way out of the wilderness. Submitting whole heartedly, we become willing to say "Yes Lord, I'll go anywhere, I'll do anything, I'll be anything, I'll carry any load, I'll live anyplace you want me to live, I'll say what you want me to say and do what you want me to."

Once we are willing to say these things, God will reveal His perfect will and we can say bye-bye moments of feeling lost, because we have obeyed His will! Therefore, the best option is to *"Present your bodies as a living sacrifice, holy and acceptable to God, which is your spiritual worship? And you will know what is that good and acceptable, and perfect, will of God" (Roman 12:1).*

We must know that the Bible contains 95% of God's proclaimed will, and for our lives to get 100% of the benefits when living by it. This does not mean we will be sinless, because no one is; but it does mean that we are willing to put away the sin in our lives as God shows us.

Then we can transform into the image of Jesus Christ in all areas of our lives, set free to receive more truth. These revelations will not come to us if we do not obey Him and we will not have peace failing to apply these keys in our lives. We need someone who has walked the path and made it safe for us to have confidence in the way to go, like the sheep trust the Shepherd. David said that *He will lead me in paths of righteousness for His name sake" (23:3) and* that is a promise!

He does it because His name is on the line and He cannot be disputed. It is His character, and His reputation that is at stake and His Word will never return void. His name is faithful and He will only lead us the right way, *"Yea, though I walk through the shadow of death, I fear no evil; for thou art with me; thy rod and thy staff they comfort me" (23:4).*

The Shepherd leads the sheep back to safety through the darkness and moving shadows. Being in the presence of the Lord gives, us comfort and we have no fear of evil because Jesus Christ is the Good Shepherd. Jesus said, *"I will never leave you nor forsake you" (Hebrew 13:5),* and knowing *"The Lord is my helper; I will not fear what man can do to me" (Hebrews 13:6),* we follow Him blindly.

LESSON

No matter what storm may come upon the path, God is faithful to guide us safely beyond what we could ever know. God has never left us in a dilemma to suffer forever; the blood of the Lamb of God is against that. Every time there is an attack of adversities, God rescues us and there is no reason to fear. *"Your rod and your staff comfort me (23:4),"*

The rod is a club that is used to drive away predators, and it is a tool used to protect the sheep from harm. The staff is a long pole with a hook on the end and aids the sheep; the crook hooks around the leg of a sheep to pull him from harm. The staff also keeps the sheep on the path that the Shepherd is leading them to by gently tapping the side of their bodies.

Understanding how the Shepherd tends the sheep illustrates the nature and character of the Lord. The Lord will never just let us wander away from His care, but helps us to stay on the path; He comforts us and supplies our every need. God pours out His love and will reprove, correct, encourage, and instruct us in a path of righteousness to protect us from Satan, the enemy of our soul. Our adversary is working through this world system to destroy us and Jesus said, "he's a liar and murderer" who lurks on our path to devour us. The devil is real and the Lord uses the club of His Word to drive Him out of our lives *"Therefore submit to God, resist the devil and he will flee" (James 4:7).*

Let us not be amiss of our other enemy the flesh that must be chasten and subdued as any other enemy against us by the word of God, so let us seek safety and, *"Draw near to God and He will draw near to you. Cleanse your hands you sinner, and purify your hearts, your double minded" (James 4:8),* and our enemies will have no victory.

Our Shepherd is watching us closely and *"Thou prepares a table before me in the presence of my enemies; thou anoints my head with oil, my cup overflows. Surely goodness and mercy shall follow me all the days of my life; and I will dwell in the house of the Lord forever" (Psalm 23:5-6).* The Lord continues to provide, lead, and protect, all in the presence of the enemy because, *"My God will supply all my needs according to His riches in glory by Christ Jesus"* *(Philippians 4:19).*

The goodness and mercy of God will follow us and pursue us, in contrast to the pursuit of David's enemies who were out to destroy him. David's desire was to go back to the tabernacle and to worship God. The mercy and kindness of the Lord is the ember to burn a raging fire of desire to worship the Lord.

We worship not always in a tabernacle, but as Jesus said, *"In Spirit and in Truth"* *(John 4:24).* We worship in our inner man, where the Lord lives; then we see that God is truly our Good Shepherd who feeds us, protects us and leads us to still waters forever! Our only response acceptable to God is holiness.

V

God Values His Children

My heart will only be at peace with Him and I believe that I am created to love the Lord, and nothing, and no one else, will do. I have been called to the high place way upon a mountain, far from all things that are not bliss, *"And He went up on the mountain and called to Him those He Himself wanted" (Mark 3:13).*

I remembered the voice of the Lord saying, He would teach me who He is, and it may have not influenced me, as it should have at that time. His Words resonated in my soul and this time I really listened to what His words were, He had said, "I'll teach you who I am." God wanted me to stop thinking, shut my mouth, open my heart and wait on His approval in my silence.

The Holy Spirit revealed to me that I needed to learn to worship and to know God, and then I would be teachable. I expected to learn and *"If anyone has ears to hear let him hear" (Mark 4:23),* and I heard Him say "you" are the school; I want you to go to. How could I be a school? Immediately I had failed the first test just like that. I began to struggle in my spirit to be what He said. I heard the emptiness hit the bottom of my belly falling short of His glory.

I had to obtain grace to go on without trying to take myself there. Oh, God help me! It saddens me to know my flesh is like a winter coat on the hottest day in the spirit. I had to take it off; there was no good thing in it! I needed to learn to worship God in Spirit and in Truth like God said, and I need Him to do it.

"Quietly" my spirit spoke, and I began to feel the coolness of the anointing of peace. I could not be more amazed at God, who is a wonder in my life. "This is the seat of mercy, a place set high in the Spirit, close to me so you can hear my voice clearly," He said, I am always here to help you; do you want me to help you?

"Behold the Lord is my helper!"(Psalms 54:4). I shouted out a praise of thanksgiving "Yes, yes, Lord I want you to help me," suddenly, all the things I felt I could never do, were already done. *"The Spirit of the Lord is up-*

on me, because He hath anointed me to preach the gospel to the poor; He hath sent me to heal the brokenhearted, to preach deliverance to the captives, and recovering of sight to the blind, to set at liberty them that are bruised, to preach the acceptable year of the Lord" (Luke 4:18-19).

His mercy is in my soul and I am holy. He said, "Wherever I send you it is holy, because I am holy and I am with you." From the day, I was born and every day of my life, I have the power of the anointing of God. He wants to teach me who He is and I am the school because the Kingdom of God and His Holy Spirit are within me.

The Kingdom of God is within me by obedience through to the Holy Spirit who is there to perfect me in being holy and righteous. God is a Spirit and I must worship Him in the peace and quietness of my love. *"Let the moderation be known unto all men. The Lord is at hand. Be careful for nothing; but in everything by prayer and supplication with thanksgiving let your requests be made known unto God. And the peace of God, which passes all understanding, shall keep your hearts and minds through Christ*

Jesus. Finally, brethren, whatsoever things are true, whatsoever things are pure, whatsoever things are lovely, whatsoever things are of good report; if there by any virtue, and if there be any praise think on these things" (Philippians 4:8).

God is offering me to come into the knowledge of who He is and I am the building that the Teacher dwells in, the Temple of the Holy Spirit. The only way to get into the classroom is to get out of the self- inflicted detention known as "My Way." Daily I soar in the Spirit released from the bondage of my flesh, which I have chosen to crucify daily!

The Shepherd's Seat Experience is the front row of the School of the Holy Spirit where He empowers me to be a child of God, and the revelation of His presence matures me to become God's holy daughter, servant and friend. Jesus said *"But when the Comforter is come, whom I will send unto you from the Father, even the Spirit of truth, which proceeded from the Father, He shall testify of me" (John 15:26).* I receive Him now in the depths of my heart as my helper, the Paraclete, sent by the Lord Jesus to guide me to all truth. He will guide me everywhere I am supposed to be and I will be given the things only of God.

He has a plan for all matters from the throne itself to direct my path. I seek Him first instead of leaning on my own understanding, in this way I know He'll get all the glory, *"Eyes hath not seen, nor ears heard, neither have entered into the heart of man, the things which God hath prepared for them that love Him" (1 Corinthians 2:9).*

I have favor with God not because I love Him so much, but because He first loved me so much. He's giving me understanding of the things He has spoken in my spirit, and *"God favors a just man" (Proverbs 12:2)* it's a spiritual principle of the Kingdom of God.

I am assured victory in the preparation of my spirit to stand before Him because it is through my obedience to Him that God blesses me. God is not obligated to show favor, *"But God hath revealed them unto us by His Spirit; for the Spirit searches all things, yea the deep things of God" (I Corinthians 2:10). Thank you Lord. Selah!* Hallelujah! The Holy Spirit is a Spirit of Revelation, now it is time to learn to listen and be quiet. The reason why we do not know more than we know is that we have refused to listen to the Holy Spirit, our beloved Teacher.

The Word of God states, *"But the anointing which ye have received of Him abides in you, and ye need not that any man teach you; but as the same anointing teaches you all things, and is truth, and is no lie, and even as it have been taught you, ye shall abide in Him"* (1 John 2:27).

My blessing is that in the fullness of Him that indwells inside of me; I am a living school of The Spirit of Truth. God has promised to give us directions in matters of daily living if we seek Him. If we earnestly look to Him for guidance, He will not allow us to make a mistake and *He will lead us in the way that He knows is best for us.*

At times, things may not always seem to be working out as we think they should, but if we will keep our trust in God, things will ultimately work out for our good. We are armed with His truth and even more equipped to sit humbly under the teachers God has placed in our life. Teachers inspired by God are incorporations of the anointing but the Holy Spirit is still the one that teaches us through one another. When we hear the word taught, the Holy Spirit bears witness with our spirit if the teaching is right, and a representation of the greater works Jesus promised.

Praise God for revealing His will, and now expect the mighty move of the Lord to oversee our lives. The Bible says, *"Verily, verily, I say I unto you, he that enters not by the door into the sheepfold, but climbs up some other way, the same is a thief and a robber. But, He that enters in by the door is the shepherd of the sheep. To Him the porter opens; and the sheep hear His voice: and he calls His own sheep by name, He goes before them, and the sheep follow for they know His voice. And a stranger will they not follow but will flee from him: for they know not the voice of a stranger"* *(John 10:1-3).*

So many Christians have been defeated because they neglect to develop a conscious contact with the indwelling of the Spirit. He manifests himself as a divine personality, living within us as a heavenly being and the Holy Spirit. God shows us how to unlearn all the things that hinders us from a deeper walk through His teachings. Our minds have no conceptualization of the way God does things and sticking our noses in God's business is not a good idea.

The outcome leads us to use logic to rationalize the lust of the flesh, however, we can rise above our human nature and to mature into God's nature. As we submit and become a witness to what thus said the Lord, *"Thy word have I hid in mine heart, that I might not sin against thee" (Psalms 119:11)*, all will be well with thee!

PRAYER

Father, thank you for sending your Son Jesus Christ as my Lord and my Savior. Through His help, I can rise above the lusts of my heart. Let your perfection be my perfection and your holiness be my holiness. I claim victory over my lust, in the name, and by the power, of Jesus Christ. All spirits of the lust of the flesh die in the Name of Jesus.

I confess that when I was supposed to be listening to the Holy Spirit I was only hearing myself. I now walk in the Spirit to the front of the classroom in which the Holy Spirit is my teacher ready to be quiet and learn. I am a child of God walking and helping others to do the same! "What, *Know ye not that your body is the temple of the Holy Ghost which is in you, which ye have of God, and ye are not your own?"(I Corinthians 3:16).* My problem was that I was still trying to be on my own accord, thinking more of myself than I ought to. Lord I repent! Please forgive me, for I loathed my flesh to dust and ashes. Amen!

Now just praise the Lord because He is worthy to be praised and He has done great and marvelous things. This is a qualification for the Shepherd's Seat Experience, being a visible manifestation as a son/daughter in the glory of the Lord.

The Shepherd's Seat Experience is our spiritual growth magnified in the knowledge of the Lord. It is every-thing that we receive as vessels of holiness engaging in the gifts of the Holy Spirit as life itself. It is everything that has the blood of Jesus applied to it, and is protected and loved by our Lord! It is more than we could ever fathom or attempt to express it is more than anyone except God knows. It is all God's glory in the Shepherd's Seat Experience. It is what Jesus Christ had while on earth to attain that same position for us. It is what He is doing right now as our Chief Intercessor and High Priest on the right hand of the Father.

We certainly may think these moves of God are just an occurrence as believers, and we acknowledge them, but, with a causal attitude. It is more than what is in our own spirits; it is a master plan of divine intervention from God to allow us an opportunity of eternity. It is the Shepherd Seat Experience, God's love sent from heaven, bringing every trial and test needed to shake us from each level of unawareness of Him as the center of life. It is the "actual" awareness of our Creator who has created us to live, move and have our being in the Living God. Only God could have designed the idea to incorporate old raggedy "hard-headed" people like us as sons/daughters under His reign.

The gates of hell cannot prevail, no matter what. We are His, and the human race has not failed, there is still hope in Jesus. The blood of Jesus has set us free and we are no longer outside of the Holy place. We can enter in freely, and as often as we like, to worship Him in Spirit and in truth. Looking back to our fore-parents, we can learn from our precious lessons of what to do so that God will be pleased. Adam and Eve turned their backs on God and added another clause into their lifestyle, "sin," which God never intended for us to have.

We are the products of generations of people who have obtained another choice by deceit of the enemy. Of course, our parents made a bad decision, and it has been going on even to this day. In all actuality, there is no other choice. God is still in control and we will all face Him one day no matter what choices we make.

The deception of the devil has blinded a whole world about the knowledge of God as the center of everything. The wisdom of God kept us alive to accept the challenge of telling the serpent to get behind us. What makes this difficult for many to accept is that Satan has penetrated the very nature of man. He has deceived humankind into believing that there is no such thing as the "devil." Now man responds more to "self-centeredness" and ignores *God centeredness* in a battle against God. The proclaimed will of God lets us know that *"The thief comes not, but to steal, and to kill, and to destroy: I Jesus am come that they might have life and they might have it more abundantly" (John 10:10).*

Jesus came down from glory to handle the matter and take back the steering wheel of our lives by destroying the works of the devil. It is the development of our character back into the original plan of God's perfection. The Holy Spirit revealed to me that this work is the Shepherd's Seat Experience; it is the preparation of true holiness as long as we are on earth, and it is, work in progress.

Each time we grow in grace and in the knowledge of the Lord Jesus Christ, we get closer to His image He desires of us. The prize of the high calling is to release that last vapor of our will and disappear in total obedience and harmony with the Lord. Becoming one with the Lord is "The Shepherd's Seat Experience" and He is sitting on the throne. God has placed a maze of grace inside of us to give us a way out in the seasons of testing. We will be tried, to see if we are truly His and worthy to sit with Him.

He has given us a way to achieve this through the Holy Spirit. We are God's perfect workmanship; blessed to be the head and not the tail, above not below, to grow in His will (Deuteronomy 28:13).

In maintaining the knowledge of whose we are, we believe that we are a spirit with a soul that lives in a body and nothing more than that. Spiritually, it is our choice to grow towards the perfect oneness with our Creator as the center of life.

"Nay, in all these things we are more than conquerors through Him that loved us. For I am persuaded, that neither death, nor life, nor angels, nor principalities, nor powers, nor things present, nor things to come. Nor heights, nor depth, nor any other creature, shall be able to separate us from the love of God which is in Christ Jesus our Lord" *(Roman 8:37-39).*

LESSON

Completing daily journeys into the heart of God, we began to mature as His temple. He is our only reality and He is perfecting us to be holy and hold on to the tangible aspect of His likeness in all that we do. The Holy Spirit imparts the intangible likeness of the Spirit of God's divine nature directly from the heart of God and places it into ours.

We are quite valuable to God. That is why He created us to share His joy in everything; especially in Him being God and God all by himself. He gave each of us a particular aspect of His joy that is specifically ours and it is up to each of us to find it; no one else can have our blessings. I am unique to God with a fresh personality from the mind of the Lord. No one else can have what God has created for us personally.

We are the manifestation of a distinctive aspect of God's nature, therefore when God looks at us; He is stimulated to move in such a way no one else can achieve. That is awesome to know God places the value of His perfection in us and it brings Him joy. Moreover, the joy we each feel in my heart is the joy God feels in His heart. We are parts of God's heart, and it is beating to perfect us with every melodic beat, drawing us into the Holy of Holies where He is, on the Throne of His own heart.

We belong to Him and we can only return pre-packaged, sealed and delivered, to go back to Him. We can never be separated from the Lord; it is not possible. We are carved in the palms of His hands. Holiness is necessary to achieve and it is the key factor to open our eyes to see Him; there is no other way!

VI

JOY, JOY, JOY

I am the joy of the Lord as I lean in closer to see who calls me by my spirit. My relationship with the Lord is based on being made spirit, soul and flesh. My flesh is a part of the physical world God placed me within to become perfected into His image.

It is by His Spirit inside of me that teaches me all that I will ever need to know about both worlds. I belong eternally to only one and by my faith, I freely choose the Kingdom of God. I possess the perfection (maturity) of God to overcome the physical world's aspect of sin through the Holy Spirit who gave me the power to become holy.

In the process, I attained the joy of the Lord in heaven, *"This I say then, walk in the Spirit, and ye shall not fulfill the lust of the flesh. For the flesh lusts against the Spirit. And the Spirit against the flesh: and these are contrary the one to the other: so ye cannot do the things that ye would. But if ye be led of the Spirit, ye are not under the law" (Gala-*

tians 5:16-18). This makes me valuable knowing I am a wonderful creation unique and one of a kind in this world; I cannot be replaced but I can be perfected through holiness.

I am distinctive in the universe fashioned by God to share the joy of the redeemed; God will restore the flawless work of His original plan.

I represent a *child of God* translated from darkness into the Kingdom of God as a new creature. The goal of the Kingdom of God on earth is to regain the tree of life that was lost in the Garden of Eden. The perfect Adam and Jesus can be understood comparing the tree of life in the Garden of Eden with the tree of life to be restored in the Last Days.

Adam was supposed to become a tree of life, and so was all of his offspring. The fall of Adam hindered our perfection, which is the will of God; ever since then the hope to be restored as trees of life, is ever present. Fallen people can never restore themselves fully as a tree of life like God planned. When I was caught in the snare of the world I could not free myself, the more I tried the worse things became. Only Jesus was able to set me free, *"And when I passed you by and saw you struggling in your own blood, I said to you in your own blood live! Yes, I said to you in your own blood live! (Ezekiel 16:6).*

He is the only one in creation who has completed all the steps to the tree of life. He came to engraft all people unto himself; Jesus is the tree of life portrayed in the Bible. If Adam realized the ideal of perfection symbolized by the tree of life in the Garden of Eden, as Jesus symbolized the tree of life in the Book of Revelation, they would be identical in the sense of having realized the goal of creation, as such, they would have equal value.

A fully mature person is perfect as God is perfect with the same divine nature of God, and is infinitely precious to the Lord. God is an eternal being, and a person created in His likeness will have eternal life also. There is no greater value than that of realizing the divine purpose of creation. Jesus obtained the greatest value as the firstborn and He was the man who has fulfilled the purpose of creation and gave us a way to our inheritance. God's divine purpose was to *"Let this mind be in you, which was also in Christ Jesus: who, being in the form of God, thought it not robbery to be equal with God. But made himself of no reputation, and took upon Him the form of a servant, and was made in the likeness of men: being found in fashion as a man, He humbled himself, and became obedient unto death, even the death of the cross" (Philippians 2: 5-8).*

"For there is one God, and there is one mediator between God and men, the man Christ Jesus" (1ˢᵗ Timothy 2:5). "For as by one man's (Adam's) disobedience many were made sinners, so by one man's (Jesus) obedience many will be made righteous" (Roman 5:19). "For as by man (Adam) came death, by a man (Jesus) has come also the resurrection of the dead" (1ˢᵗ Corinthians 15:21). "He has fixed a day on which He will judge the world in righteousness by a man whom he has appointed" (Acts 17:31).

Jesus came to show us the unique character of God's perfection through rebirth into the Kingdom of God. When Phillip asked Jesus to show him God, Jesus said,

"He who has seen me has seen the Father; how can you say, "Show us the Father?" Do you not believe that I am in the Father and the Father is in me?" (John 14:9-10).

The Bible says, *"He was in the world, and the world was made through Him, yet the world knew Him not" (John 1:10). Jesus said, "Truly, truly, I say to you, before Abraham was, I am" (John 8:58).* Jesus is the Son of God, born to complete the purpose of creation, which is eternal life and He is the First Born.

The Bible refers to Jesus as the Word made flesh *(John 1:14),* He is the incarnation of whom the Word became alive. The Bible states that all things were made through the Word and that the world was made through Jesus. *(John 1:3, 10).*

The Lord intended for each of us to attain perfection through the fulfillment of our responsibility as mature children of God. In our fallen nature, we have no connection to God; He cannot use us for His purpose as children of disobedience. Jesus paved the way and placed value back on the human race; we are the redeemed and *"All* *things are put in subjection under Him" (1st Corinthians 15:27).* Sin stained the relationship God had intended to have with us and Satan came in, and has been attacking us ever since. Jesus came and had no original sin; He had no condition in Him that the enemy could attack. As a fallen man, we were blind to the heart of God.

However, Jesus not only understood them fully, He also lived it. The Shepherd's Seat Experience teaches us to reach for this same fullness, to be holy and acceptable in the sight of God, and have life more abundantly. The Father wants none of us to perish, that is how great He is, and we are valuable to God personally.

Jesus broke through the stain of sin and provided us with the opportunity to approach the Lord. He died on the cross to save humanity and His blood delivered us from the evil of eternal death. We now have an Intercessor in heaven explaining all the details of our flaws to the Father.

Christ is the head of the church *(Ephesians 1:22),* and we are His body and members *(1st Corinthians 12:27).* Jesus is the main temple and we are branch temples. He is the vine and we are the branches *(John 15:5)*. We are the wild olive shoots to be engrafted with Jesus; the true olive tree *(Roman 11:17)*. Accordingly, Jesus called us "My friends" *(John 15:14)*, and it is written, *"When He appears we shall be like Him" (1 John 3:2)*. Jesus is the first fruit and those who believe in Him are to become the next generation *(John 3:3)*.

The Lord gave us life for His glory, to learn how to sit comfortably within the Shepherd's Seat Experience. God is setting up a day that He will rebirth a new creation with Him as the center. This is the purpose that Jesus has been exalted and His bride (the church) as the second parents, a new Adam and Eve to become the true parents of humanity.

Through Jesus and the Holy Spirit, people of faith are being rebirth into the spiritual family of God. Christ will return and He will be expecting His bride to consummate on earth the perfected union of God..."*And then shall appear the sign of the Son of man in heaven: and then shall all the tribes of the earth mourn, and they shall see the Son of man coming in the clouds of heaven with power and great glory" (Matthew 24:30).* The original sin of man will be erased and the new creatures (us) will be able to enjoin in the everlasting fellowship with the Lord as the center of all things.

This will truly be the Kingdom of God and we are waiting in developmental stages of its full manifestation here on earth. Thus, God is constantly asking to be our Lord totally and completely.

TESTIMONY

It is incredible to meditate and listen to the guidance of the Holy Spirit. He tells me that it will not be long before I can sit up straight in the seat of my heavenly destination. I long await the fullness of God; I hate the attachment that sin has placed on my life. Sometimes it seems like a computer that working fine; and then gets a virus. It then begins acting up even though it has been programmed to work effectively. Paul said it so well, *"When I want to do right I do wrong and if I want to do right and I don't; it's the* virus of sin living in my computer (me). I want what is right, which is correction and reproof in my life, I cannot face life's obstacles on my own, and I do not have too.

The Father did a great and mighty act of love when He gave us Jesus *"For God so loved the world He gave His only begotten Son, that whosoever believes in Him should not perish, but have everlasting life. For God sent not His Son to condemn the world, but that the world through Him might be saved" (John 3:16).*

He is our plan of salvation to get us out of the mess we made by making friends with the enemy. The best that I can do is to believe in Jesus Christ as my Savior and allow the Holy Spirit to continue to inspire me to walk in the His light. I know I must be cleansed both physically and spiritually to obtain the complete transactional result of the cross. Being transformed by the renewal of the spirit of my mind (into the image of God) after the initial rebirth is the divine order of God. God is uniting His Kingdom back unto himself. This is "mind-boggling" and I am a witness to God awesome power with no dispute.

LESSON

No one can stand in the way of the hand of the Almighty God El Elyon, the creator of all things. His call for action displayed in Jesus Christ has finally come to decree and declare the glory of the Lord forever. We as a community of believers must come together with this awareness.

We must begin to experience the Shepherd's Seat Experience as an assembly of the Church. We must learn to be *one* again with the Father through Christ Jesus. The joy of the Lord awaits His faithful followers.

VII

WHAT ARE WE TO DO?

"Fulfill my joy, that you be like minded having the same love, being of one accord, of one mind"(Philippians 2:2)

To fulfill something is the assurance of that which has already been promised, predicted or foreshadowed and obtained. To complete something is to make it whole by including every part that is wanted. God knows joy and wants His people to know joy. He is rejoicing over the redeemed people whom He has called to be His "joy."

What is this joy of the Lord? The joy of the Lord is being holy and standing before Him in love, meeting the expectations He has set for our lives. We can trust God's word and have an overflow of confidence in Him, and be inspired in the gift of being His joy.

The joy we experience in our Christian lives is a direct reflection of our walk with the Lord. What does your reflection look like? Remember to *"Rejoice in the Lord and again I say rejoice" (Philippians 4:4).* We must keep our faith in on Jesus, *"the author and finisher of our faith"* *(Hebrews 12:2)*. We must maintain that, *"Now faith is the substance of things hoped for and the evidence of things to come"(Hebrews 11:1)*.

Let yourselves be the joy of the Lord, be His champions by trusting Him, *"But without faith it is impossible to please God, when you come to God you must believe that He is and that He is a rewarder of them that diligently seek Him"(Hebrews 11:6)*. Jesus' work on Calvary guarantees that we each will finish the race with victory and ultimately you will be exalted according to God's grace and favor.

"Be joyful always; pray continually, give thanks in all circumstances, for this the will of God for you in Christ Jesus"(I Thessalonians 5:16-24). God will turn all our sorrow into joy; however, we must meet His expectation first. The condition is that no matter how horrendous or tormenting the circumstances afflicting our souls, God says that He is making *"Everything work for the good of those who love Him and are called according to His purposes through Christ Jesus"(Roman 8:28)*, *"Who for the joy set before Him*

endured the cross. Scorning its shame, and sat down at the right hand of the throne of the Father" (Hebrews 12:2).

The Lord Almighty, who spoke the heavens into existence, left glory and humbled himself, taking on flesh and blood to save us from sin. The Creator became the creation, by assuming our identity as man, and took all our sins on himself who was sinless. The Master's plan had the great expectation that we would assume His identity and become holy.

Jesus Christ is the Son of God. He died on the cross for our sins and rose on the third day with all power over heaven and earth. When we ask Him to come into our lives, He forgives us of our sins; that is the joy of the Lord. We then become like Christ, righteous and Holy, enabled to obtain and sustain joy in the life we have chosen.

When the Father looks at us, He no longer sees our sin; He sees the blood of His Son Jesus Christ in our place. Jesus Christ, fully God and fully man, understands the sorrows we suffer; He also knows the joy of suffering is always at the end. God's faithful followers know that *trou-*

ble will not last always and that it should be endured. Just remember, you must go through the sorrow to birth the joy, be patience as our glorious Savior has shown us in His bitter death.

To suffer for Him, we will have that seat He holds for us on the right hand of the Father; being with Him in sweet victory. God is speaking to the poor, the hungry, the weeping, and the rejected people to come to Him and find the peace they seek. God will fill your hearts with the joy and make you whole, *"If ye then be risen with Christ, seek thou things which are above, where Christ sits on the right hand of God. Set your affection on the things above, not on the things on the earth. For ye are dead, and your life is hidden with Christ in God" (Colossians 3:1-3).*

God knows all the conditions of your life and He reminds us of the story in the Bible of Job and the patience he maintained through great affliction. The name Job means *"the persecuted one"* and most of us know how it ended....Job lost everything; his family, his property, his prestige, his possession, his friends, and no one could help him. It may have seemed onlookers, that he should just throw up his hands and give up, but *"Blessed are they which are persecuted for righteousness sake; for theirs is the Kingdom of heaven. Blessed are ye, when men shall revile you, and persecute you, and shall say all manner of evil against you falsely, for my sake. Rejoice, and be exceeding glad; for great is your reward in heaven: for so persecuted they the prophets which were before you"* (Matthew 5:10-12).

Through all the anguish, Job trusted God and endured and his faith brought him joy at the end of his suffering. Suffering is a part of life and when those dark days show up and it seems as if God has forsaken you.

Nevertheless, remember God will sustain and restore your life as He did Job's. God is faithful to us, despite our shortcomings and our inability to understand what is happening. He knows the beginning and end of every situation. Give Him glory and thank Him in all circumstances. Shout for joy, because He is setting up His Kingdom to share His eternal joy with you.

Being in alignment with the will of God is having an acceptable relationship with the Him and is the fruit of this joy. The grace of God's alone manifests it and not man's own efforts. It is a state of delight and well-being coming from knowing and serving God.

Joy is God centered and can only be obtained and sustained by Him, and is available forever. However, self-seeking is enslavement which often leads to the vicious cycle of ungodly things because there is no satisfaction obtained. God commands His people to convey the opposite experience of those who are shut out of the Kingdom.

Those who do not heed to His commands will suffer the anguish of separation from God, their experience will be that of utter darkness, weeping and gnashing of teeth. The joy of the Lord enables us to enjoy all that God has given us. The point is that God wants us to know the joy as a celebration of life. We are blessed to be able to share the joy and the sorrows of life with one another. The Word of God says to *"Rejoice with those who rejoice and weep with those who weep" (Romans 12:15); "Count it all joy" (James*

1:2). You will be rewarded for all the heartache and pain you have endured so *"Be not deceived; God is not mocked: for whatsoever a man soweth, that shall he also reap. For he that soweth to his flesh shall of the flesh reap corruption; but he that soweth to the Spirit shall of the Spirit reap life everlasting. And let us not weary in well doing; for in due season we shall reap, if we faint not" (Galatians 6:7-9)*.

LESSON

This is a day that the Lord has made let us have joy in it. Let go of your sorrows because the Lord has commanded all sorrows to be joy, and in the end is peace. Go ahead and praise Him anyway!

VIII

THAT'S JOY!

The storms of life rage through our existence and we think it is over. We encounter all types of adversities and our backs are against the wall. People around us seem to begin to leave us when we need them the most, and it appears that all is hopeless.

Nevertheless, God says, *"I'll never leave you nor forsake you"* thus, your hope is in the Lord; that is joy. You may be in so much pain that you may have even tried to numb the feelings of loneliness, anger and got yourself strung out on drugs. God says, "if you trust me I'll deliver you", and that is joy.

Unemployment is the highest it has ever been and many are experiencing economic pitfalls, losing and have lost their families, homes and some have lost their minds. People everywhere are wondering "how am I going to make it?" God says that He is your provider and that is joy. God has not forgotten, He knows your conditions and wants you to believe in Him; not your circumstances. God says, *"hold on to my glory because, those who mourn shall be comforted" (Matthews 5:4), and "Be ye transformed by the renewal of your mind" (Roman 12:2).*

Experience the fruit of the joy of the Lord; devote yourself to what God wants, wait on Him in the storms, don't get weary and don't faint. Give God the praise and serve the Lord with joy and humility. Love Him and with gladness, He will never let the mighty waves of the sea of trouble overtake you because He is greater than the mighty waters and crushing winds of adversity.

He will not let your boat be destroyed and will guide it safely to shore. The condition of this promise is that you must love Him with all your heart, soul and strength. Love is our distinction from others, and when we love, it is living the life God has called us to do.

Having the same love is a motivation from God to experience Him as the source of all joy; it is the Shepherds Seat Experience magnified. Pray for God's blessings and thank Him for His love, patience, the Spirit "love" and showing us how to cultivate it *(Galatians 5:22)*. *"Therefore we also pray that our God would count you worthy of this calling and fulfill all the good pleasure of His goodness and the work of faith with power"(II Thessalonians 1:11).*

Jesus loved us so much that He gave up everything in glory and became a servant, just so we could know which way to live. What are you willing to give up for God today? Lying, cheating, stealing, sexual immortality, and all the works of the flesh. Sin is what is keeping you from the joy of the Lord and a path to holiness and righteousness.

You must change the way that you live because Jesus said that you had greater works to do. He must increase, and you must decrease! Stop complaining it is stealing your joy! Every time you complain, you say that the problem is bigger than God's love.

Be a blessing to one another, love as God has commanded and wait on the Lord. The Lord is the Father of lights and the giver of all good gifts, wait on the promises of the joy of the Lord. Hate what is evil and cling to what is good that is evidence of Holiness *"For the Lord is faithful, who will establish you and guard you from the evil one, and we have confidence in the Lord concerning you, both that you do and will do the things we command you. Now may the Lord direct your hearts into the love of God and into the patience of Christ" (II Thessalonians 3:3-5).*

Get deliverance and change your attitudes today, be like David, a man after God's own heart who loved and did not kill "Saul" (your enemy) even if you have an opportunity. Remember the battle is not yours, but is the Lord's, let it go and *"Recompense to no man evil for evil. Provide things honest in the sight of all men. If it be possible, as much lieth in you, live peaceably with all men. Dearly beloved, avenge not yourselves, but rather give place unto wrath: for it is written, vengeance is mine: I will repay, saith the Lord. Therefore, if thine enemy hunger, feed him; if he thirst, give him drink: for in doing so thou shall heap of coals of fire on his head. Be not overcome of evil, but overcome evil with good" (Romans 12:17-21).* Be like Moses, go up the mountain to see what God wants, but do not come down the same way you went up. Be in the presence of the

Lord like Mary Magdalene, and sit at His feet and be transformed by His Words and *"And be not conformed to this world but be ye transformed by the renewal of your mind, that ye may prove what is that good, and acceptable perfect will of God" (Roman 12:2).*

Be like Ruth who thought more of others than herself and found the joy of the Lord in her humility. Imagine Peter's feelings when he denied Jesus the first time, then the second time and finally the third time.

Peter did not let his circumstances defeat him he sought out new possibilities; he kept on pressing towards the mark of the high calling. Look at the joy each of these believers whose sorrows were great but not greater than God's power.

Trust God who is faithful, loyal and just, and experience the joy of the Lord. *Stand up and jump for joy in the Lord!* Now we are standing in the overflow of the manifested presence of the Lord. Shout joy and dine on His daily bread, which is joy for the spiritually hungry soul Let the spiritually thirsty souls drink from His living water of joy. Exemplify restoration of the soul, and recovery of sight to the spiritually blind, be of one accord. Do not believe in the crisis in your life but believe in the Christ in you; live holy and acceptable.

He has promised to overthrow pain and suffering into joy. Hold on to the glory of the Lord and you will bear fruit! Believe that God can do exceedingly and abundantly above what you have asked Him. The ways of the world are meant to imprison you with an ungodly self-centered mind to stealing your joy of the Lord.

Keep your eyes on Jesus all the time and be confident that His joy has consumed all sorrows. Jesus is the light that has broken into darkness; His love has overtaken hate to bring peace. Today you have absolute victory in everything you do, so follow what God has commanded *"Fulfill ye my joy, having the same love, likeminded, being of one accord and of one mind" (Philippians 4:4)*.

Live beyond the cross with a resurrected life, rise from every dead situation in your lives and rejoice in the Lord. Repent, child of God, and prosper in the overflow of the presence of the Lord; every yoke is destroyed, every strong hold pulled down and every burden is lifted. The anointing of the Lord is operating in your heart right now and you are healed and delivered in the Name of Jesus. God has made your enemy your footstool today, and given you power over their works, *"Greater is He that's in you then he that's in the world" (1 John 4:4)*. The day of the Lord is fast approaching so be ready filled with the *"Fruit of His Spirit love, joy, peace, faith, gentleness, goodness, meekness, longsuffering and temperance"(Galatians 5:22)* and Enter into the joy of the Lord.

LESSON

Accept no substitutes, and do not be denied what is rightfully yours! Make a joyful noise unto the Lord. Worship and praise Him through the "good" times and the "bad" times. Finish your course dancing in the glory of the blood of Jesus. Let everything that has breath praise the Lord. Worship Him and bless His holy name; He deserves the highest praise; oh magnify the Lord with me. Trust in the Lord's power at all times, not those ungodly people, places or things set to destroy your joy. Say thank you Lord. Now shout for joy!

IX

I

AM

QUIET!

When Moses came down from Mount Sinai with the two tablets of the testimony in his hands, he was not conscious that his face was radiant because he had spoken with the Lord. The people were afraid to come near him, Moses called to Aaron, all the leaders of the community, and they came back to him.

When Moses spoke to them, he put a veil over his face. However, when he entered the Lord's presence to speak with him, he removed the veil, *"And when he came out and told the Israelites what he had commanded, they saw that his face was radiant. Then Moses would put a veil back over his face until he went to speak with the Lord"(Exodus 34:30,34-35).* Glory to the Lord for He is God! Many times the people around you will be afraid to come near you because the glory of the presence of the Lord has manifested in your radiance (anointing).

It is the mighty and powerful work of the indwelling of the Holy Spirit, so be encouraged to move forward. We are redeemed and no longer have to seek God as it was done in days of old. He lives inside of each believer. We cannot do anything without the help of the Holy Spirit and God is calling us to total surrender in Him.

The Holy Spirit makes it easy for us to surrender as we quieted our spirits and listen to God. Without the Holy Spirit, we would never have that nudge to push on no matter what. As we wait on the manifestation of the Lord, we are filled with His Skekinah Glory.

People will look at you and tell you that you are glowing. They can see the radiance of God's Skekinah Glory emanating from your being. It comes with the total surrender of self-centeredness and engaging in the Lord as the center of your being. When we empty ourselves, God fills us with His excellence through our obedience. The people who encountered Moses were burned by the glorious presence of the Lord, and their lives were changed. It is a wonderful tribute when people see the glory of the Lord on our faces; their hearts are turned to God.

We can fully recognize that we are doing the things of God and the light of His glory cannot be hidden. Yes, we make a bold statement without uttering a word that we are in the presence of the Lord Himself.

God gives Christians today this same Skekinah Glory of the Old Testament to those who stand on holy ground with Him. The Bible says, *"For God, who said, "let light shine out of the darkness" made His light shine in our hearts to give us the light of the knowledge of the glory of God in the face of Christ (II Corinthians 4:6).*

This wonderful light is the glory of the residence of the Holy Spirit coming through, evidenced to all since Jesus *"Was life, and that life was the light of men"* (John 1:4) The Lord Jesus, working with the Holy Spirit, gives light (truth), which is the holiness of God. We need the Father, the Son and the Holy Spirit all wrapped together to find the joy that results from being present with Him. When we let go and relinquish our spirits we receive the Skekinah Glory of worshiping the Lord. The Skekinah Glory is with us in the world today, and is available to all who believe and battle for holiness.

The Israelites had only the Word of God when they came out of captivity in Babylon. When they heard it, they received it and went on their way with the joy of the Lord in their hearts. They realized that they could not take stock in material goods and they should still be joyful for being; to be with God is to be empty of the world and all that it contains. The Israelites had the Feast of the Tabernacles, which honors God as the host and them as the guest.

We must come to believe in the living presence of the Most High God within us and rejoice in it as the Israelites did in having His Word. We must have faith in to worship God and the radiance of the Holy Spirit lets everyone know that we are His. It is a reflection of the love of Jesus written all over our faces, it is the light of Christ shining through as the power of creation itself. Receiving this power makes us think differently, act differently, and people respond to us differently. When the Gentiles heard the good news of the Gospel, they rejoiced, praising and giving thanks to the Word of God, and they were glorified.

They were filled with joy because it came from the praise of the Lord; praise changes our "inner being" and then we have true joy. It is a blessing to receive the glory of the Holy Spirit, we need to take pleasure in Him and treasure Him daily.

LESSON

We witness to others about how wonderful God is for giving us, His Skekinah Glory, so they may burn with a desire for Him also! And *"May the God of hope fill you with all joy and peace as you trust in Him, so that you may overflow with hope by the power of the Holy Spirit (Roman 15:13).*

YOU ARE GLOWING!

X

THE BATTLE FOR HOLINESS

We have been delivered from the authority of sin by Jesus' death on the cross as we have learned in previous chapters. Sin is always present and is daily trying to take us over. Apostle Paul said, *"When I want to do good, evil is right there with me" (Romans 7:21).*

We will continue to have these struggles because sin is present in the world. What God does is equips us to learn how to handle sin His way. The more we realize that it is there, the less it can affect us and we will despise and fight against it.

Believers have a proclivity to sin, the Holy Spirit maintains within us a prevailing desire for holiness because *"Whosoever is born of God does not commit sin, because he is born of God" (1 John 3:9).* By the Word of God, believers are enabled to see themselves and the sin that will cripple them. In this light sin is exposed as an enemy to God; it also distinguishes believers from unbelievers who stay in the darkness of sin. As Christians, we can all identify with Paul's statement, *"When I want to do good evil is right there with me."* Indwelling sin remains within us even though it has been dethroned. It has been over thrown and weakened, but it still has the same nature because sin is hostile to God's ways and cannot submit to Him *"Because the carnal mind is enmity against God: for it is not subject to the law of God, neither indeed can be" (Romans 8:7).*

This result is a relentless enemy of righteousness right in our own hearts and diligence and watchfulness is required of us. We must wage war against this enemy by learning everything we can through the Word of God about the nature of sin and its tactics.

Scriptures indicates that the seat of indwelling sin is the heart, *"For from within, out of men's heart, come evil thoughts, sexual immorality, theft, murder, adultery, greed, malice, deceit, lewdness, envy, slander, arrogance, and folly. All these evils come from inside and make a man unclean"* (*Mark 7:21-23).* It is coming from within our own "heart" and we will find in the scriptures this term is used in many different aspects; it often means our reason or understanding; sometimes our affections, emotions, sometimes our will; and it can represent the whole soul of man with all its faculties.

The "heart" is the origin of a person's total inner control tower of their character and their desire to pour out goodness or evilness from within them. Simply stated, it is our perceptions, thoughts, reasoning, intentions, purpose and our faith; it is the mind as it reasons, discerns, and judges the emotions as something we like or dislike. The conscience as it determines and warns, and the will as it chooses or refuses, are all together the heart.

The Bible says, that the heart is deceitful and unsearchable to anyone but God alone, and that *"The heart is deceitful above all things, and desperately wicked: who can know it? I the Lord search the heart, I try the reins, even to give every man according to His ways, and according to the fruit of his doings" (Jeremiah 17:9-10)*. Believers are saved but "we" still don't own our hearts *"But with me it is a very small thing that I should be judged of you, or of man's judgment: yea I judge not mine own self. For I know nothing by myself; yet am I not hereby justified: but He that judges me is the Lord. Therefore judge nothing before the time, until the Lord come, who both will bring to light the hidden things of darkness, and will make manifest the counsels of the hearts: and then shall every man have praise of God" (1 Corinthians 4:3-5).*

We all have hidden motives that we do not realize in our hearts; none of us is immune to the fact that there is an enemy within us. We cannot fully search out this adversary to battle, the heart is deceitful, and it excuses, rationalizes, and justifies our actions to please its yearnings.

Sin blinds us to entire areas of unrighteousness in our lives and we only use half measures to correct these aspects, because we cannot search our own hearts fully. We should proceed with caution concerning our own hearts; we need to ask the Lord daily to look at our hearts and show us the sin in it. We are unable to see within our hearts and maybe we do not want to see it. David's prayer is suitable for each of us, *"Search me, O God, and know my heart, test me and know my anxious thoughts. See if there is any offensive way in me, and lead me in the way everlasting"* *(Psalms 139:23-24).*

How does God search our hearts? God searches our hearts by way of His Word. As we read it under the power of the Holy Spirit, *"The Word of God is living and active. Sharper than any doubled edged sword, it penetrates even to dividing soul and spirit, joints and marrow; it judges the thoughts and attitudes of the heart." (Hebrews 4:12).*

We must continue to stay in the Word of God that exposes our heart to be searched by the Holy Spirit. If we try to search our own heart, we will be discouraged by what we find logically; it will deceive us and tell us that our hearts are not the issue.

The adversary will attack us and try to make us feel God will not accept us because we are sinners, and then we will not battle for holiness and remain in the dark hopeless. It is only by the Holy Spirit, searching our heart by the Word of God, which enables us to see the gray areas of our lives that we are in bondage. Our unsearchable hearts is the seat of indwelling sin and we should not get it twisted; it is our own evil desires that makes us rebel against the Lord.

Remember, Adam and Eve listened to their own heart more than God's, and we are now in the midst of that same storm. Fleshy desires are strong forces that must be controlled during temptation so we will not get pushed over the edge. The reasoning of the Holy Spirit indwelling must step in and help us in the struggle. What happens then becomes the spirit against the flesh and the flesh against the spirit.

Who will win? If our desires win, we looked away from God and gave in to the temptation. This world's system caters to our desires and tempts us into conforming to the world's view. This is known as the "pleasure of sin" and *"Choosing rather to suffer affliction with the people of God than to enjoy the pleasure of sin for a season" (Hebrews 11:25)*. Fortunately, as believers, we desire what God wants first hopefully; however, we must take heed because we have both good desires as well as evil desires. Great examples of these good desires include our desire to know Christ *(Philippians 3:10)*, a desire to see others saved *(Romans 10:1)*, a desire to birth spiritual children who grow and mature in the Lord.

It is the bad desires that lead us to sin and we are dragged away by our own evil desires into temptation *"But every man is tempted, when he is drawn away of his own lusts, and desires" (James 1:14)*. We only have ourselves to blame when we fall, because we have the Holy Spirit that tell us only the truth to follow.

*The issue is "it's you "*and we become the problem by yielding ourselves into our own temptation. We only have victory in the battle for holiness as we mature and gain control over our lustful desires through obedience. It is by our own evil tendencies to sin, and not an external variable, that we respond to when tempted.

Stop blaming others for your shortcomings. Repent and continue in the way of righteousness. Temptation is always searching for the evil desires of the heart for satisfaction to enter into. Recall a particular temptation in which you are weak; notice how often you find yourself thinking of ways to satisfy those demons. It leads us into playing with them and engaging our appetites towards them.

Indwelling sin is such that even if we confess the sin, we may still find ourselves thinking about it all over again. This may create another avenue for temptation to pop up suddenly; it is easy since it has already been brewing in our hearts. If you put paper into a fire it will burn, this is how our evil desires respond to temptation.

In this battle for holiness, our desires must always be towards God. He is able to keep us from falling; seek to glorify God and not the lusts of the flesh and we become steadfast and unmovable. Indwelling sin will attack our reasoning and understanding, leading us to believe that what is wrong is right.

The Word of God admonishes us to resist the devil and *"That ye put off concerning the former conversation the old man, which is corrupt according to the deceitful lusts; and be renewed in the spirit of your mind" (Ephesians 4:22-23).*

We have all been *"Deceived and enslaved by all kinds of passions and pleasures" (Titus 3:3).* These passages talks about the "old man" but let us not forget that this same deceit still wages war against us, however, it can never overtake us. What happens first when we are deceived is that little by little we begin to fall away from watchfulness, and then from obedience.

We become like Ephraim, of whom God said, *"Foreigners sap his strength, but he does not realize it. His hair is sprinkled with gray, but he does not notice" (Hosea 7:9)* . We fall away from watchfulness by taking things for granted and we come to believe we are beyond a particular temptation. We look at someone else's fall and deny that we are able to fall in that area.

Let us be warned by Apostle Paul who states, *"If you think you are standing firm, be careful that you don't fall"* *(1 Corinthians 10:12).* Even when we are helping someone who may have slipped, we must be careful not to be tempted as well. God's word reminds us *"Brethren, if a man be over taken in a fault, ye which are spiritual, restore such a one in the spirit of meekness; considering thyself, lest thou also be tempted" (Galatians 6:1).*

Many times, taking things for granted, we fall away and abuse God's grace *"Who change the grace of our God into a license for immorality" (Jude 4).* We abuse God's grace when we continue to sin and think it's okay because we are forgiven by claiming, *"If we confess our sins, He is faithful and just to forgive us our sins, and to cleanse us from all unrighteousness" (1 John 1:9).* Shall we continue to sin? Of course, not, so stop playing with the Lord!

We fall away from obedience when we start to doubt God's Word. This is how the serpent deceived Eve; *"Now the serpent was more subtle than any beast of the field which the Lord God had made, yea, hath God said, ye shall not eat of every tree of the garden? And the woman said unto the serpent, We may eat of the fruit of the trees of the garden; But of the fruit of the tree which is in the midst of the gar-den, God hath said, Ye shall not eat of it, neither shall ye touch it lest ye die. And the serpent said unto the woman, ye shall not surely die; for God doth know that in the day that ye eat thereof, then your eyes shall be opened and ye shall be as gods, knowing good and evil" (Genesis 3:1-5).*

The devil is still a liar, and just as he said to Eve, *"You shall not surely die"* and he also speaks lies to us saying "It is only a tiny thing and God won't notice it." Yes God will, because *"The eyes of the Lord run to and fro throughout the whole earth to show himself strong on behalf of those whose heart is loyal" (II Chronicles 16:9).*

Sin cannot overtake us; however, it does wage an onslaught against us, and if we are not careful, it will defeat us by deceit. We must always have our mind under subjection to the whole armor of the Lord Jesus Christ.

We stand firmly and move swiftly in our battle against indwelling sin, when we nip our ungodly desires in the bud. Resist the devil and he will flee is a promise of the Word of God according to the book of James, Chapter 4 verse 7.

It is all for our benefit when we take heed! We have the guidance of the Holy Spirit and *"When the sentence for crime is not quickly carried out, the heart of the people are filled with schemes to do wrong" (Ecclesiastes 8:11),* we will do what God wants instead! There is always a battle with the flesh's lustful desire and we must not forget this fact; our hearts are unsearchable, our evil desires are insatiable, and our thinking is always in danger of being deceived.

That is why our Lord Jesus told us to *"Watch and pray so that you will not fall into temptation" (Matthew 26:41).* Solomon warned us *"Above all else, guard your heart, for in it is the wellspring of life" (Proverbs 4:23).* Our thoughts are valuable when we think good thoughts, and our mouths will speak the things of our heart; good people have good things in their heart.

LESSON

Our heart is what we are always working with; it is the center of our spiritual life development. If we find ourselves in discourse, we must go to the root of the disturbance, which would be within the heart. If there is a tree with bad fruit, we do not try to fix the fruit we go to the root to find the problem. The heart of the problem is the problem of the heart's wickedness.

Test your heart today, what happens if someone accidentally bumps into you? Do you become angry? Do you curse them or bless them? This is how we know what the state of our heart is by our response to others. What is the state of your heart? Are you still complaining about your life or comparing it to others?

Are you walking in love and delight of the laws of the Lord? Do you love the Lord as you say you do in action? What happens when you see someone who is dirty, smelly and talking to themselves? Do you call them crazy? Do you lead them to Christ? If not, what is in your heart?

Are you offended easily? Are you a backbiter? Do you delight in others unhappiness? Are you still holding a grudge? Are you slothful to the works of the Lord? Thank God, that if you are suffering from any of these heart conditions, Dr. Jesus can fix every one of them. He is waiting to cleanse us from all forms of unrighteousness and to show us compassion, love, understanding and acceptance, in hopes that we will learn to do the same.

God's Word will heal us and help us to stay grounded in the matters of the heart. In order to see the Lord, our hearts must be purified and true to Him only. Pray and again ask for deliverance, and He will give you an inside job as He gave David.

"Create in me a clean heart God and make my spirit right again" (Psalms 51:10). Be in the blessing and not the curse, the light and not the dark, in prosperity and not famine in the name of our Lord and savior Jesus Christ to whom all the glory is due. "Now unto Him that is able to keep you from falling and to present you faultless before the presence of His glory with exceeding joy" (Jude 24).

XI

THIS IS AN INSIDE JOB!

Dressing up the outside will not fix your heart problems; pretty clothes make you look nice, but they do not help you to live right. Big cars and fine homes give you status, but they do not give you eternity; these things only last for a little while. Here is the situation at hand, the outside appearance is shining like new money; but as for the interior, where the heart is, and there is only darkness.

The outside altered, but the inside faltered. Which side of the road are you on? The choice is always yours to *"Enter ye in the strait gate; for wide is the gate to destruction, and broad is the way that leads to hell and many there are going in; strait is the gait, narrow is the way which leads unto life and few find it by their fruit"* (Matthew 7:14). The fruit of your heart will produce the Fruit of the Spirit in your life. God's joy is the uniting of your heart with His; you will delight in the things of the Lord and you will be victorious! Hold on to what God says is right; and not what your evil desires tell you; the devil is out to destroy your relationship with God. We can call God ABBA or Father and He will come and help us out whatever is harming us. God will never tempt you with evil *"Therefore if anyone is in Christ he is a new creature, old things have passed away; behold all things have become new (II Corinthians 5:17).*

God has delivered us from the realm and reign of sin through the competed work of the Lord Jesus Christ at the cross. We were in the bounds of sin, like slaves, we were committed to our evil master and the pleasure of sin. We developed sinful habits regardless of how *"good"* we were and on a sentence of death. Nevertheless, our Lord Jesus Christ came into this sinful world and took our place on Calvary.

He died to sin and through our union with Him, we died to sin also. Now we are free from the authority of sin in our lives. No more slave mentalities, we believe that we have the power to resist the devil and by doing so, he flees.

Sin has no claim on us, but it still lives within us, and it is constantly trying to trip us up into sinning, but we can still live holy lives. Yes, Jesus defeated sin once and for all through His death however, we will be tested, harassed and even defeated in our hearts by sin.

Some may ask, *"What good does it do to try to live holy?"* We just have to accept the fact that God is still in control; He is wise and knows the plans He has for us, and it is not the gates of hell. God has delivered us from the overall reign of sin. If we trust Him, we are dead to sin and alive in Him.

We no longer walk in darkness but in the marvelous light of the Kingdom of God, *"Being then made free from sin, ye became the servants of righteousness" (Roman 6:18)*. What is the implication of being alive unto God? How does it help us in our pursuit of holiness? United with Christ and all His power; we are unable to live a holy life without Him. We are not called to faith to do our "own thing" as Christians, to decree and declare the will of God. *"Not that I speak in respect of want: for I know how to abound: eve-*

rywhere and in all things I am instructed both to be full and to be hungry, both to abound and to suffer need. I can do all things through Christ which strengthen me" (Philippians 4:11-13).

Paul is speaking about being content with the circumstances we are in, whether it is plenty or in want, hungry or on full. It is through the strength of Jesus Christ that we can do all things. This applies to holiness because our reaction to the circumstance is a part of our holiness. We have to conform to the character of God and be obedient to His will. Be content no matter what the circumstances look like, we must be holy.

The Bible says, that we are *"Strengthen with all power according to His glorious might so that you may have great endurance and patience" (Colossian 1:11).* And, *"That out of His glorious riches He may strengthen you with power through His Spirit in your inner being" (Ephesians 3:16), "God is able to do immeasurably more than we ask or imagine, according to His power that is at work with us" (Ephesians 3:20).*

We are alive unto God; He is all the strength and power that overcomes every bit of infraction against Him. Sin causes us to have a sense of hopelessness by its power over us, and many times we resolute not to do a certain thing, just to find ourselves doing it anyway. It is true we need God to overcome all these things; *we cannot do it alone* is a key principle with noteworthy value.

Knowing that we cannot accomplish anything without the power of God, gives us the will to overcome and resist temptation. Our power is in Christ because of two facts; first, we are dead to sin and its authority over us. Secondly, we are alive in God, united with Him and His strength is always with us through His Holy Spirit.

When we internalize these facts, it takes us away from the sense of hopelessness. The reasons why we feel these emotions are because of the terrible power of sin, and the way it works is like this: We lose our sense of hopelessness by letting go and allowing the power of God to reign in our hearts against sin. Sin then loses its authority because God cannot be defeated, and we are with Him in victory; we cannot be defeated. Even though we are weak, God is strong evidenced by us getting into the habit of being dead to sin and alive to God. By faith, we believe in God's Word, we resist the advance of temptations.

This is the kind of faith that keeps us from falling by holding on to the purposes God has for us *"Likewise reckon ye also yourselves to be dead indeed unto sin but alive unto God through Jesus Christ our Lord" (Roman 6:10).* We have the power of the Holy Spirit living inside of us because we are of God.

The Holy Spirit guides us to live the life God wants for us. The Bible teaches us *"But ye are not in the flesh, but in the Spirit, if so be that the Spirit of God dwell in you. Now if any man have not the Spirit of Christ, he is none of His. And, if Christ be in you, the body is dead because of sin; but the Spirit is life because of righteousness. But if the Spirit of Him that raised up Jesus from the dead dwells in you, He that raised up Christ from the dead shall also quicken your mortal bodies by His Spirit that dwells in you" (Roman 8:9-11).*

Because the Spirit of God is working within us, it makes us able to act according to God's good purpose. The choice is up to us to choose to live for the Lord and have faith in Him; it's the only way to please God, *"For it is God which works in you both to will and do of His good pleasure" (Philippians 2:13), "God did not call us to be impure, but to live a holy life. Therefore, he who rejects this instruction does not reject man but God, who gives you His Holy Spirit" (1 Thessalonians 4:7-8), God gave us the Holy Spirit to shows us how to live holy. We are temples of God "Flee fornication. Every sin that a man does is without the body; but he that commits fornication sins against his own body. What? Know ye not that our body is the temple of the Holy Ghost which is in you, which ye have of God; and ye are not your own?" (1 Corinthians 6:18-19).*

We are not controlled by our sin nature but by God's Spirit within us, *"But ye are not in the flesh, but in the spirit, if so be that the Spirit of God dwell in you. Now if any man have not the Spirit of Christ, he is none of His" (Romans 8:9), "This I say, walk in the Spirit, and ye shall not fulfill the lust of the flesh" (Galatians 5:16).* **We have the Holy Spirit living within us to give us the power to live holy.**

This makes us subjects in the Kingdom of God, united with Christ by His Holy Spirit who lives within us. The Holy Spirit shows us our need to be holy; He enlightens our understanding so that we begin to see the plans and purposes of God for us to become holy. He makes us aware of sin in our lives, and the devil works hard to keep us blind spiritually so we cannot see where we fall short.

LESSON

"The heart is deceitful above all things and beyond cure. Who can understand it?"(Jeremiah 17:9).

God knows your heart, so stop fooling yourselves; repent in the name of Jesus. Go and sin no more, continue in the way of righteousness and acts of holiness for the glory of the Lord. AMEN!

XII

The Heart

Thank God, for not placing the responsibility to and expose the hearts of man on themselves; only the Holy Spirit does this. We must be led by the truth in order to accept the things we can change. Walking in the midst of our own accord, we would be lost in self-deception; we need the Holy Spirit's guidance.

Leaders in the church must recognize that they are not exempt and can be deceived about indwelling sins. Leaders must take heed and guard against falling into what they preach for others to live by. Teaching the scriptures is not living the scriptures and without the application of the will of God, we are only deceiving ourselves.

How many opportunities have we met with conviction about our sins but did nothing about it? God will not allow us to be ignorant to the devices of the adversary James says we are deceiving ourselves. *Stop fooling yourself "But ye are doers of the word, and not hearers only, deceiving your own selves. For if any be a hearer of the word, and not a doer, he is like unto a man who beholding his natural face in a glass; for he beholds himself and goes his way and straightway forget what manner of man he was. But whosever looks into the perfect law of liberty, and continues therein, he being not a forgetful hearer, but a doer of the work, this man shall be blessed in his deed. If any man among you seems to be religious, and bridles not his tongue, but deceives his own heart, this man's religion is vain. Pure religion and undefiled before God and the Father is this. To visit the fatherless and widows in their affliction, and to keep himself unspotted from the world." (James 1:22-27)*

LESSON

A doer of God's Word continues in the work of the Lord with full responsibility and not let it just tickle their ears. Doers implement God's Word by action, thought and deed to accept the challenge to transform themselves by the standards of God's Word! The Word of God states, "Let him with an ear to hear what the Spirit says to the Church" is indicative of obedience.

How can God do the good work in us, if we only hear the Word and not act upon it positively? Self-deception creeps in when we will not do what is necessary to change to glorify God, we become a "cast away" as Paul describes, caught up in the wrong things acting as if they are right. Action is the key that God has given us as believers; it transforms us into the image of God.

Those who are only hearers and not doers of the word will not see the Kingdom of God because they do not have a pure heart and clean hands! The work we do in the Name of Jesus witnesses to others for the glory of the King! Our faith in Him is alive which means the work in the Kingdom starts in our own heart. We are, blessed by our commitment to the Lord and we are set free *in* this world but not *of* this world!

We know that being a doer of the word means we can do all things in Christ who strengthens us. We desire to see the advancement of the Kingdom of God on earth and in our hearts. The battle for holiness is obedience to the Word of God, the will of God, and the ways of God, all requirements of the Shepherd's Seat Experience. As Leaders, we must have total and complete faith in our Creator to become holy.

Thank the Holy Spirit who reigns over our lives by our faith in the Lord and our repenting heart *"Even so faith, if it have not works, is dead, being alone" (James 2:17)*. Nothing we do is profitable without the Holy Spirit, who directs and instructs us how to live, move and have our being in the Lord. Christian leaders must continue to exercise their faith and believe God! God promised that we would see the reward of the wicked with our own eyes.

All believers must have that *"now"* faith to overcome all the things that tries to divert us from serving the Lord. Our primary purpose is to commit to the sentence of eternal life and extend ourselves humbly.

Faith is the essence of who we are in Christ and works are not separate items from our faith used individually unless our labors fail. Let this spiritual concept influence your daily life. Remind yourselves that if we say we love the Lord, and do nothing, we lie.

139

How can we allow sin to run rampant in our lives and never try to change? He said, "The sheep of my pasture know my voice and they follow." The Holy Spirit will empower us to carry out the mission of Jesus in our lives and the lives of others. We stand only on the Word of the Lord and seek His counsel in all that we do. We then will maintain our pure hearts and clean hands to serve Him first in our own lives.

PRAYER

Lord, Father and our God, we believe totally in our new life in Jesus Christ; our heart exposed will show His work within us. We have chosen the name of Jesus for our salvation. How can we not put into actions and in deeds by faith, what you told us to do?

Our Lord and Savior Jesus Christ despised the shame of the cross for us with joy. We proceed in action and in faith and we will not operate on doctrine that alone does not save, because even the devils in hell know the Word. We will act on faith because your Word has taught us that our service is void without it. Lord, let us not fail as leaders and grieve the Holy Spirit. Open our hearts and show us the unrighteousness that keeps us from walking closer to you. We love you Lord and we want what you want for us. Lord, you are so good and we follow you willingly.

Obedience is far better than sacrifice and we will obey your Word. No sin can overtake us for we are not alone and we are in Christ dead to sin and alive in Him. Our assurance and confidence is in your Word, you told us that *"No temptation has overtaken you except such as common to man: but God is faithful, who will not allow you to be tempted beyond what you are able; but with the temptation will also make the way of escape that you may bear it "*(I Corinthians 10:13).

Lord we believe you and we trust you to complete the work you have started within each of us forever. Thank you Father, you are the mighty God and we place our trust in you in the name of Jesus! Holy Spirit have your way. Amen.

XIII

HUMILITY

"James, a servant of God and of the Lord Jesus Christ, to the twelve tribes which are scattered abroad, greeting. My brethren, count it all joy when ye fall into diver's temptations; knowing this, that the trying of your faith works patience. But let patience have her perfect work, that ye may be perfect and entire, wanting nothing. If any of you lack wisdom, let him ask of God, that gives to all men liberally, and upbraided not; and it shall be given him. But let him ask in faith, nothing wavering. For he that wavers is like a wave of the sea driven with the wind and tossed. For let not that operate think that he shall receive anything of the Lord. A double-minded man is unstable in all his ways. Let the brother of low degree rejoice in that he is exalted. But the rich in that he is made low; because as the flower of the grass he shall pass away" *(James 4:1-10)*. Humbling ourselves before the Lord, we know by faith that He will lift us up; submitting ourselves wholly and freely to the ways of

the King of kings. He will exalt us in ways we could not have performed on our own. This is a *reflection* of a personal relationship with God. We should think of ourselves like Mary Magdalene, at the feet of the King waiting for His command.

We should want to be humbled in all degrees towards Him having nothing to do with pride or arrogance; many people suffer greatly for this cause. Keep your eyes on the prize by humbling yourself and know that matters of the heart are worked by the Holy Spirit.

The blood of Jesus was shed for us to be justified, sanctified and washed clean. God is clear in His Word that the unrighteous shall not inherit the Kingdom of God. Some people say that they believe in the Lord, but they are liars because they do not live by His statures.

Do not give the devil any place by believing that you can operate in faith without working out your own salvation with fear and trembling; there is work to do. The Word of God reigns in our lives, or we are deceiving ourselves practicing a form of godliness by denying His power in our lives! Faith pleases God and produces good things. A lack of fruit in one's life according to the Word of God is because of a lack of faith. Jesus has paid the full cost of our cleansing.

The Word of God gives us faith and the power to do the good works that produces fruit of the Holy Spirit in our lives. *"Wherefore let him that thinks he standeth take heed lest he fall" (1 Corinthians 10:12).* Ignoring what is righteous and not being led by the Holy Spirit, we are in trouble with God and wandering in the wilderness of our mind, body, soul and our spirit; never knowing the benefits of serving the Lord...*"Wherefore the rather, brethren, give diligence to make your calling and election sure; for if you do these things, ye shall never fall; for so an entrance shall be ministered unto you abundantly into the everlasting Kingdom of our Lord and Savior Jesus Christ" (11 Peter 1:10).*

Diligence in confirming our election of God takes place in our spirits. Can we ever forget that the atoning blood of Jesus Christ has washed us clean? It would not be easy if we did not make sure of it by the sanctification process, and participate in the divine election of God. Our expectations are in the Lord to do great and marvelous things all for His glory.

Perfection is all about giving God all the glory for our lives by trusting His infinite wisdom. It happens, as we understand that God moves according to the plans He has for us and not the plans we have for Him, so do not be dismayed. God already has a plan for your life, which trumps our feeble wantonness and makes a way out for us.

God desires to prosper us and sometimes what we desire is not conducive to those plans or His will; He blesses us with something even more valuable. God's demonstrations are alive in the Bible of Him doing just that, recall the story when Peter and John were, on their way to prayer.

They came upon a lame man crippled from birth who was carried daily to the temple gate called Beautiful; he had been a beggar at this place for many years. He saw Peter and John and asked them for alms. Peter looked him

145

straight in his eyes and so did John for they were traveling together. Peter told the man to "look at us" to captivate his attention to heal him as he saw Jesus do many times to quicken their faith.

Therefore, the beggar looked at Peter and John and his expecting heart got more than he ever thought. The beggar did not know what to expect, but his faith was quickened. A key in receiving anything from God, we must *expect* something from Him. He gave them his full attention and they told him *"Silver and gold have I none, but as such as I have I give thee in the name of Jesus of Nazareth rise up and walk" (Acts 3-6).*

He did not receive the riches of silver and gold; Peter offered him the gift of eternity in the name of Jesus Christ of Nazareth. The minute Peter had the man's attention; he did two things, first he admitted his lack of material wealth and that he could help him there.

Secondly, he showed him how rich he was in the spiritual realm and commanded him to walk. By the authority of the Holy Spirit and in the name of Jesus of Nazareth, the lame man received power to walk. His feet, and his bones were strengthen enough to support his weight for the first time in his life. In this electrifying moment while looking at one another; and in the name of Jesus, something remarkable took place.

Peter reached out taking him by the right hand, he helped him up and he walked. Peter depended on the power of the name of Jesus when he told him "I don't have silver and gold" that is not what you really need; let us not diminish the fact of this beggar's need for money, food and clothing.

That was not what Peter had to offer him; he had the integrity and the power of the name of Jesus coming through him at that time. What we glean is that the Lord is saying "look at me" with great expectation to receive His blessings. We must transform by the power of the Holy Spirit, and stop begging the world for our provision and depend on the Lord! His testimony was fulfilled and his feet was shod with the preparation of the Gospel of Peace (*Ephesians 6:15*) as he jumped and jumped praising God.

He went into the Temple to tell everyone; he entered into the gates with thanksgiving and now he went into courts with praise *(Psalms 100:4)*. He had been empowered to be a witness for the Lord and he told everyone about His goodness. His testimony amazed and filled the people with wonder. However, they only remembered him as the lame man at the gates begging for alms.

They would never release him from a begging state to a rejoicing state; not everyone will acknowledge our transformation. The world is blind and cannot see the new creatures that we have become; all they will see is the same old lame beggar.

Be encouraged and see your face reflecting in the eyes of the Lord on your behalf! The gate called Beautiful is truly the opened heart to the transforming power of God. God is waiting to transform our lives from the crippling states of the flesh and fill us with His Holy Spirit and *"I have never seen the righteous forsaken nor his seed begging for bread (Psalm 37:25)*. The begging is over, trust God with expectations; with your full attention. He is looking directly into our lives to bless us in ways we never ex-pected. The blessing he gave the unsuspecting lame man, and because of the miraculous restoration he received, he became a witness of God. True witnessing always follows a pattern.

First God works; He does something only He could do and man cannot do. Then man explains what God has done for him to others, and then the pattern starts over again. Every day we live is a miracle; we must witness it to everyone that crosses our beautiful gate, our clean heart the hope we have in God. Think of how overjoyed this man was; he had never known love, joy, respect, dignity and self-worth.

When the Lord shows up, He restores and renews eve-rything; the lame man found out that he was worth more to someone then a few dollars; dignity and respect cannot be brought. The Lord gave him power to walk in His glory and never beg the crumbs of the world. God desires us to live a life with great expectations, which only God can achieve, *"The outward man perishes, but the inward man is being renew day by day" (II Corinthians 4:16).* He now had a personal relationship with the Lord; he found Jesus who was the solution and completion to all that troubled him in his life.

LESSON

As we walk in this life, let us be restored to wholeness and ask the Lord for help. Ask in wisdom and then we will discover the real value of God's purpose for us. God will always get the glory, but it is better for us that we give it to Him first in praise and thanksgiving.

Peter and John were able to use their holiness for His works. Each of us has to be ready to use our spiritual wealth to give others in our holiness. The church has not been called to meet the material needs of the world; but has been called to meet the spiritual needs of the world.

The parable of the good Samaritan keeps us in balance, and shows us that we can help people with our money. However, the church is not responsible for doing that; the church releases the will of God. The church makes spiritual growth and development available to all who desires to be whole. God will make them holy and acceptable in His sight, by faith and in the Name of Jesus. Let us walk into every situation and take authority and God will strengthen us where we are weak.

We will be able to withstand the weight the world cast upon us. Stand up and walk home to glory! We know that the Lord will never give us a burden too heavy to perform; our holiness is a miracle to the world. God designs frustration, delays and setbacks to strengthen us to change into what God wants. Have you been saved for years but your life displays little difference from the time you made your confession to Christ? Could it be that you have never given God your full attention?

We will all experience changes in our heart when we meet God on hallowed grounds. Sadly, some have never expected to receive anything even when they go to church. The minds of the young and old are turned off in church service sitting there thinking all sorts of things, taking mental trips and playing mental games. Unfortunately, they arrive and leave missing the power of giving God their full attention; allowing distraction to be the center of their worship. We attend services on Sunday morning, but who is attending our minds?

The devil uses distractions to steal our deliverance from us right there in church. Ask yourself "Where has my mind wandered while I was in church service?" Unfortunately, the life changing truth going forth from the Word of God passes right by people in church and they come and leave with no expectation. They will not hear the Word of God and will not transform. We must give God all that we have all the time; without expectation, there are no miracles.

If we keep, our hearts opened and our eyes on Him we will receive more than we expected. God will give us all that He planned for us before the foundation of the world and add no sorrow to it. God is saying to each of us "look at me" and *"He that has an ear let him hear, let him listen" (Matthews 11:15. 12:9. 13:42) (Mark 4:9, 4:23, 7:16) (Luke 8:8, 14:35).* We must be ready to profess our holiness in everything, giving God all the glory; there's a crowd of people called the world watching us heal the lame; give them something they may not expect, the integrity and deliverance in the name of Jesus Christ. The Lord has said *"Be ready always to give an answer to every man who asks you for a reason for hope that is in you, with gentleness and courtesy" (1 Peter 3:15).*

EXPECTATION

I command you in the name of Jesus of Nazareth to rise up and walk out of depression, generational curses, bitterness, resentment, backsliding, family problems, unemployment, drugs, fear, pride, arrogance, an unforgiving heart, adultery, fornication, lack of faith, loneliness, selfishness, all manner of illness and whatever is hindering your spiritual growth and be filled with the Spirit of the Lord.

Receive the power to tread upon the head of serpents and scorpions; the power to tread over all your enemies and no harm shall touch you, *(Luke 10:19). Be transformed by the renewal of the spirit of your mind! "Make every effort to live in peace with all men and to be holy: without holiness no one will see the Lord" (Hebrews 12:14). In the Name of Jesus! AMEN!!*

XIV

Obey God!

Believers are living in an unholy world where sin is the status quo, they face temptation daily. Jesus taught at the Sermon on the Mount that God's Word regulates our outward conduct and our inner disposition. It is not enough that we do not kill as an honor to God, the giver of all life, we must also not hate.

It is not enough that we do not sleep around; we are not to even think about such evil. We must learn to bring the appetites of our flesh under control in thoughts, deeds and actions. Everything that concerns us must be under subjection to the Lord Jesus Christ.

Our thought life marks our character, and whatever we think about rules who we are, *"For as a man thinks so is he" (Proverbs 23:7)*. It's because of our thought patterns that Paul said, *"Finally, brothers, whatever is true, whatever is noble, whatever is right, whatever is pure, whatever is lovely, whatever is admirable, if anything is excellent or praise worthy, think about such things" (Philippians 4:8).*

As Christians, we are no longer to be conformed to the pattern of this world but we are to transform into the likeness of God, by changing our thinking to such an extent that it is the mind of Christ and not ours. Allowing the Word of God to internalize into our lives, we transform and it becomes a total and complete part of who we are.

Anyone can be a chameleon conforming to every environment encountered by him or her without a preference to any, but only a child of God can transform into the likeness of God that never changes! Follow the Word of God *"And be renewed in the spirit of your mind" (Ephesians 4:23) and experience this glorious exchange "As obedient children, not fashioning yourselves according to the former lusts in you ignorance" (1 Peter 1:14), "I beseech you therefore, brethren, by the mercies of a living sacrifice, holy and acceptable unto God, which is your reasonable service. And be not conformed to this world: but be ye transformed by the renewing of your mind that ye may prove what is that good and acceptable, and perfect will of God" (Romans 12:1-2).*

156

Through our union, with the indwelling of the Holy Spirit, we are holy because He is holy purged of our former sins and assured to never fall. The choice to transform and not conformed to the ways of this world creates an intimate relationship with the Lord.

We belong to Him who made us for His good pleasure whereby we have His peace. This acknowledgement allows us to rest in Him and to learn who He really is. We can have the peace that He will be Jehovah Jireh, our great provider of all; we have happiness, and His joy.

This attitude of happiness is not only satisfaction, it is the evidence that God is with us, and we desire to put away the things of the world. It is at the forefront of our lives as we search for higher ground; the Holy Spirit will place them in their proper perspectives. This achievement aligns us will God's perfect will, as the Holy Spirit moves to cleanses every heart of those whose hope is in the Lord.

We are alive in the Lord and have the courage to keep pressing toward the high calling in Christ Jesus. Inner joy may not mean a thing to some people because they are not alive in Christ. Furthermore, even as these words are forming, so is a weapon of destruction against them. The weapon is their refusal to do self-examinations to make sure they belong to God and trust His plans for them. God is serving our hearts with the notice to change and walk in the love of Christ.

God desires that we realize the joy on the outside can do nothing to help us grow on the inside. We will never have a completely joyous life unless we worship God with a heart that trusts Him. Believing the promises of God with our hearts, and not our logic, allows us to transform from misery to joy.

The joy is the light that spreads love throughout the world by those who believe in Christ. It causes us to let God govern and direct us. God uses the restoration, recovery and renewal of His presence to give us the rest we need. Wrestling with God's will for us is useless and we become weary and faint. Moreover, letting go of personal agenda is mandatory to walk with the Lord! Then and only then will our hearts be given over to Him "for real" thus tapping into the anointing of the Lord. Holiness enables us to let go of earthly concerns and find ourselves over-whelmed with joy in His presence.

The King, the Master, the Lord is with us to worship Him and to thank Him by our faith in Him. God allows us to touch His love by coming closer to meet Him where He is by being in a state of total denial of self. God guides our hands to lift in worship to touch His face and feel the heat of His glory purifying our hands.

God has allowed us these precious moments in prepa-ration for other times when we look for Him and it seems as if we are standing alone! Periods of holy, separation baffles us as we shuffle in the Spirit looking for our Lord; without warning, He seems not to be there.

We yearn to be near Him and memories of intimate moments of His glory flood our spirits. Selfishly pouting we want to behold His splendor; but we do not know where He is. We tell ourselves that we have met Him in this place so many times before, but we forget to continue our expectation and the delight of our beloved escapes us.

Personally we want to share our hearts with Him, wondering how we could we be so full and empty at the same time. Longing for His nearness, we set out to find His embrace. The Word of the Lord says, *"All night long on my bed I look for the one my heart loves. I looked for Him but did not find Him. I will get up now and go about the city, through its streets and squares; I will search for the one my heart loves. So I looked for Him but did not find Him. The watchman found me as they made their rounds in the city. Have you seen the one my heart loves?" (Songs of Solomon 3:1-2).*

This is personal and we wonder if God heard our pleading and our tear drops falling. Yet still we sit and wait in this place on high, waiting to hear His footsteps. In the quiet, we listen to hear His Words of love, and we can feel Him everywhere, but still we cannot find him. Our memories of the last we shared, has overtaken us and we faint in the waiting of love. He *is not* listening, not coming to meet us, and not holding us in His tender arms. What is my beloved doing now? In a feeble attempt to understand the ways of God, we think and rationalize His whereabouts; thinking about where He once was to find Him.

Why has He withdrawn from us His sweet and lovely excellence? We begin to search ourselves in repentance trying to find where we went wrong. We intensely blame ourselves for His absence due to our shortcomings. What can we do to bring Him back, we contemplate? Praying in new levels of tongues, we discover our yearnings still did not bring Him back. We could not work our faith to bring us back into the presence of the Almighty Lord.

However, the Holy Spirit is our witness and our faith holds back the thought of ever being forsaken; He promised to never leave us nor forsake us. Somewhere, here in the silence, in the seemly emptiness, He watches in the hidden fullness of His glorious presence.

"Where are you Lord?" We listened back for an answer and still none came; something was going on and it was going on inside of us. Falling short of the glory of the Lord is as simple as forgetting that He is the center and not ourselves. We have learned the ways of our Lord, who is a God who hides himself and He hides himself for a purpose. Why does God do this? His purpose is only to prosper our souls and to cause us to pursue Him, not finding Him and we await His return.

God is directing us into the deep plans He has for us; He walks slowly before us in His silent glory. He makes the crooked places straight for us to pursue Him as Jehovah Shamah the God who *is* there. As believers, we will go through times of desert experiences, which are phases of testing and building foundational spiritual growth.

God calls us into a journey like the children of Israel from Egypt to Canaan. After 400 years of bondage, God let His people go; Moses took them on a journey to the promise land, by way of the wilderness. This was a journey of testing and molding an old people into a new people, an unholy people to a holy people.

This was a time of hunger, thirst, enemy threats and overwhelming monotony. Despite all the difficulties, it was a season of the manifestation of the provision of God. They were taught the nearness of God. Even when He does not appear to be, God taught them total dependence on Him. When the children of Israel responded with faith, the Lord Almighty provided His love and power.

However, the lack of the unity of faith, murmuring, and doubting made their stay in the desert longer, and some never found the Promised Land. Our seasons in the desert will not be much different for us; there are times of self-motivated anxiety between God's inconceivable nearness and the absence of so many of the comforts and provisions we normally taken for granted.

God's purpose for these times is to strip away everything we depend on for refuge and self-assurance making them less achievable. Whatever we have set up in our lives as idols will be destroyed, God does this to cleanse us of all unrighteousness; and to teach us to trust Him. We pray that all the hindrance of intimacy fall away daily, so the opening before us is the promise land of God's seal.

These will be difficult times, but when we endure we'll find ourselves maturing in the Lord. We learn there is no one like the Lord, strong and mighty. He is the provider of the water we thirst for in dry times. He is faithful to call each of us into the desert to teach us who He is and cleanse us from all unrighteousness. The desert events of our lives are places of manifestation of miracles, which meets every hindrance and defeats them before our eyes. Staying in the place where God has placed us and being content, we will see the glory of the Lord prevail.

When manipulation and mistrust are at the head of the table, we are making unrighteous agreements against the Lord; God wants us to trust Him with our lives. This may be very difficult for someone who has been hurt many times and daily re-live the fear; trust God more than your fears. God loves us and wants us to be healed and delivered, trusting Him that cannot lie to fulfill every promise to us.

LESSON

God's purpose for our journey in the desert is to purge us into adamant, steadfast faith and absolute obedience, enduring every adversity. This we experience until we know by our spirit that God is trying to provide our every need. Hold on and endure the suffering, the joy is with you now; you will soon see the light of your salvation breaking the dark clouds of suffering. *Psalms 106* offers great advice on how to respond to the desert event, which is a requirement of the Shepherd's Seat Experience.

XV

THIS IS HOW IT IS IN THE DESERT

"Praise ye the Lord. O give thanks unto the Lord; for He is good; for His mercy endures forever. Who can utter the mighty acts of the Lord? Who can show forth all His praise? Blessed are they that keep judgment, and he that doeth righteousness at all times. Remember me, O Lord, with the favor that thou bearest into thy people: O visit me with thy salvation; that I may see the good of thy chosen, that I may rejoice in the gladness of thy nation, that I may glory with thine inheritance. We have sinned with our fathers, we have committed iniquity; we have done wickedly. Our fathers understood not thy wonders in Egypt; they remembered not the multitude of thy mercies; but provoked Him at the sea, even the Red sea. Nevertheless, He saved them for His namesake, That He might make His mighty power to be known. He rebuked the Red sea also and it dried up; so He led them through the depths, as through the wilderness. And He saved

them from the hand of him that hated them, and redeemed them from the hand of the enemy. And the waters covered their enemies; there was not one of them left. Then believed they His Words; they sang His praise. They soon forgot His works; they waited not for His counsel: But lusted exceeding in the wilderness, and tempted God in the desert. And He gave them their request; but sent leanness into their soul. They envied Moses also in the camp, and saint of the Lord. The earth opened and swallowed up Dathan, and covered the company of Abram. And a fire was kindled in their company; the flame burned up the wicked. They made a calf in Horeb, and worshipped the molten image. Thus, they changed their glory into the similitude of an ox that eats grass. They forgot God their Savior, which had done great things in Egypt. Wondrous works in the land of Ham, and terrible things by the Red sea. Therefore, He said that He would destroy them, had not Moses His chosen stood before him in the watch, lest He should destroy them. Yea, they despised the pleasant land, they believed not His Word: But murmured in their tents, and hear Aaron the harkened not unto the voice of the Lord. Therefore, He lifted up His hand against them, to overthrow them in the wilderness; They joined themselves also unto Baalpeor and ate the sacrifices of the dead. Thus, they provoked Him to anger with their inventions; and the plague brake in upon them. Then stood Phinehas and executed judgment: and so the plague was stayed. And that was counted unto Him righteousness unto all generations for evermore. They angered him also at the waters of strife, so that it went ill with Moses for their sakes: Because they provoked his spirit, so that he spoke unadvisedly with his lips. They did not destroy the nations, concerning whom the Lord commanded them: but were mingled among the heathen, and learned their works. And they served their idols; which were a snare unto them. Yea, they sacrificed their sons and their daughters unto the devils, and shed innocent blood, even the blood of their sons and their daughters, whom them sacrificed unto the idols of Canaan: and the land was polluted with blood. Thus were they defiled with their own works, and went a whoring with their own inventions. Therefore was the wrath of the Lord kindled against

His people, insomuch that He abhorred His own inheritance. And He gave them into the hand of the heathen: and they that hated them ruled over them. Their enemies also oppressed them, and they were brought into subjection under their hand. Many times did He deliver them; but they provoked Him with their counsel, and were brought low for the iniquity. Nevertheless, He regarded their affliction, when He heard their cry: And He remembered for them His covenant, and repented according to the multitude of His mercies. He made them also to be pitied of all those that carried them captives. Save us, O God and gather us from among the heathen, to give thanks unto thy holy name, and to triumph in thy praise. Blessed be the Lord God of Israel from everlasting to everlasting: and let all the people say Amen praise the Lord" (Psalms 106).

Lifesaving divine principles are within these percepts to help lead us to the understanding of God's purposes during difficult, yet transforming seasons. Psalms 106 invites us to the instructions of the living God for His purpose in the seemly quiet times of our hidden Lord. We should always believe God's promises that He has made to us, for in these verses they are simple and easy to do. Learning them activates our commitment on a daily basis such as:

1. Singing Him praises (vs. 12)

2. Remember to what He has done for you in the past, seek His counsel (vs. 13)

3. Do not give in to sinful desires (vs. 14)

4. Do not envy others (vs. 16)

5. Do not turn to familiar idols (vs. 19)

6. Do not despise the place God has you in (vs. 24)

7. Don't complain (vs. 25)

8. Obey the Lord (vs. 25)

9. Do not strike out in anger (vs. 33

10. Cry out to God in humility (vs. 44)

11. Always and no matter what continue to praise the Lord! (vs. 48)

Furthermore, by following these simple instructions, we will be set free and the Holy Spirit will lead us through beastly states of wilderness in peace. God will not give you more than you can bear, so stick with the plan and manifest the Shepherd's Seat Experience within you as you learn how to be holy because, *"Blessed are those who have learned to acclaim you, who walk in the light of your presence, O Lord. They rejoice in your name all the daylong; they exalt in your righteousness" (Psalms 89:15-16).*

God is very specific about what He desires for our lives and His good pleasure. Even with such explicit instructions contained in Psalms 106 people fall to worship people. It is strange how they will give up everything for that person with an irresistible and out passion; but for God they are unyielding.

Comparing that interaction with worshipping God, we will find there is much difference. No human experience can compare to when we worship at the feet of the Lord. As we begin to see His power, excellence and grace, the countenance of the Lord is then stimulated and He blesses you. Worshiping God to the fullest allows His majesty to cleanse us of our self-centeredness. He knows every detail of His creation; His wisdom is forever; His riches are immeasurable, He is breathtaking and His omnipotent power blesses every aspect of creation. Make your commitment personal by desiring only Him in every awaking hour and as you sleep, know God's there.

God has blessed the world so richly and furnished it with everything we need; He is never too busy to demonstrate His awesome wisdom. God is infinitely above any need that we may have of Him. He is above our reach, our conceptions and we cannot comprehend Him, yet when we say yes we arrive at our ultimate existence and purpose in Him.

Entering into the presence of the Lord's Skekinah Glory, we worship Him and praising His majesty. God has imprinted purpose is our hearts desire to find His grace pouring out His offer of salvation to all men. We can't make it on our own, God is the instrument of all our being, He is *"The God who made the world and everything in it is the Lord of heaven and earth and does not live in temples built by hands. And He is not served by human hands, as if He needed anything, because He himself gives all men life and breath and everything else. From one man He made the very nation of men that they should inhabit the whole earth; and He determined the times set for them and the exact places where they should live. God did this so that men would seek Him and perhaps reach out to Him and find Him, He is not far from each one of us. "For in Him we live and move and have our being." as some of your own poets have said "we are His offspring" (Acts 17-24-28).*

The Spirit of excellence is following God's instructions, which sparks the fire of worship to praise and glorify Him. The goal of worship is not to see what we can get out of it; the goal of worship is to exalt the Lord. Worship is lovingly reflecting the radiance of the glory of God's holiness, it contains all His worth in our feebleness. Furthermore, worship is a part of us that will not be denied, it stems from our longing to be with our Father.

Being led by the Holy Spirit is the perfecting of the saints for the work in the ministry and edifies the Body of Christ. Worshiping the Lord is a bond of loyalty and a gift of love *"Therefore I say unto you, what things so ever ye desire, when ye pray, believe that ye receive them, and ye shall have them."* (Mark 11:24). The practice of worshipping God in every act opens up the gates of heaven for us to receive the blessings of God's promises. God is our spiritual lover and we should want to please Him; love Him; praise Him; delight only in Him instead of other things. What terms has God given us to do battle with the flesh?

God has provided us with every tool…*"My brethren, be strong in the Lord and in the power of His might. Put on the whole armor of God that you may be able to stand against the wiles of the devil. Take up the whole armor of God that you may be able to withstand in the evil day, and having done all, to stand. Stand therefore having girded your waist with truth, and having put on the breastplate of righteousness, and having shod your feet with the preparation of the gospel of peace; above all taking the shield of faith with which you will be able to quench all the fiery darts of the wicked one. And take the helmet of salvation, and the sword of the spirit, which is the Word of God. Lest Satan should take advantage of us; for we are not ignorant of his devices"*

(Ephesians 6:10-11,13-17, II Corinthians 2:11). The Word
of God teaches that praise and worship are constantly on
the minds of believers and in every aspect of a life of holiness.

We must continue to lift our hearts before the Lord
and search for the fire to live above the flesh and grow
spiritually. Every attitude, hunger and reaction bound in
the flesh is a hindrance to intimacy with the Lord.

How can we make it better you say? First, we always
go by what God has said, and second we resist what He did
not say because it is an attack of the enemy of our soul.
Satan does not want us to have a relationship with the
Lord because he cannot; God has shown us in His Word
how to resist Satan and he will flee.

Sometimes in our process of spiritual transformation,
we may feel that we have failed, but that is a lie to keep us
feeling guilty. The devil is an enemy and it is him whisper-
ing evil to divert us from following God's instructions.
We must be submitted to discipline ourselves to learn the
way to worshipping God.

The Holy Spirit moves through our faith and draws us closer into the presence of the Lord, and when it seems as if the winds of the Spirit does not fill our sails, don't be distressed. We have the tools God has provided to deliver us from the evil one and bring us to Himself, the Holy one. He is worthy beyond description, above reproach and His acts of redemption is an amazing exhibit of His grace.

the Lord makes a way of escape when, the devil tries to steal our praises, kill our desires and destroy our wiliness. Regardless to whatever the situation, God gets all the praise and all the glory! God has removed the limits of the evil one forever to provide us a way to keep moving toward the prize. The devil does not want us to be in the presence of the Most High God, in awe and reverence of His mysterious great powers.

The adversary does not want our praise and worship ascending towards the Father and the gates to heaven opened for us. He hates to see the glory of the Lord on our faces and in our spirits. This speaks doom unbeknownst to him as we present ourselves in the arms of the Lord in victory. God has given us our praise and worship of Him to push evil from out of our midst. His wicked ways are quite clear to us when we are in the Lord and we have the amour and weapons of defense of holiness!

God has set up a powerful arsenal of spiritual weaponry and our assurance rest in the Word of God. The Word of God created everything there is upon the face of the earth (Gen 1:3;6;9;11;14;20;24;26;29) with the words *"AND GOD SAID."* Standing on the Word of God defines what we have been given spiritually. Our walk is with Christ, and we must apply His spiritual principles to our lives personally.

We must accept our stand and declare it by the Word of God as the absolute truth *"For ye are all the children of God by faith in Christ Jesus"(Galatians 3:26).* We have been born again of the Spirit of God. We have been given much in Christ *"Blessed be the God and Father of our Lord Jesus Christ who blessed us with spiritual blessings in Heavenly places in Christ (Ephesians 1:3-4).* We have been chosen by Him before the foundation of the world, that we should be holy and without blame standing before Him in love. The qualification of the Spirit are specific, such as His holiness, grace, benevolence, power, love, patience, righteousness, compassion, faithfulness, severity, and His constant presence are all reasons to worship God. Trusting His Word qualifies us according to His terms, *"But of Him are ye in Christ who of God is made us unto wisdom and righteousness and sanctification and redemption"* *(1 Corinthians. 1:30).*

As children of God we have grace, *"Even when we were dead in sins He quickened us together in Christ, as children of God we have been made alive in Christ, raised in Christ and seated at God's right hand in Jesus Christ"(Ephesians 2:5-6).* We are complete in Him who is the head of all principalities and convicts us into correction *"As ye have therefore received Christ Jesus the Lord so walk ye with Him"* *(Colossians 2:6).*

LESSON

We are to walk as Christ, holy as children of God. To be effective we must receive Christ, *" If ye live by the Spirit* let thee also walk by the Spirit"(Galatians 5:25), "For we are His workmanship created in Christ Jesus unto good works which God hath before ordained that we should walk in them" (Ephesians 2:10).

The Word of the Lord crushes the enemy of our soul, Satan, the accuser, the serpent, murderer, destroyer, thief, wolf in sheep's clothing and angel of light. He invites the people of earth to stand with him in darkness. He wants us to believe him and not the Lord. God has equipped us with everything we need to stand against him.

In order to worship and praise God effectively we need to understand who our enemy is, *"Our struggle is not against flesh and blood but against dark forces" (Ephesians 6:12).* The enemy is not the people around you even though they have used you despitefully and hurt you! Our real struggle is not against any particular person who has wronged us. Our real struggle is against our own feelings of bitterness and frustration. God tests us during these attacks of the enemy in hope to find us confessing of faith in Him.

To initiate deepen adoration of the Lord we must surrender every aspect of our personality, logic, emotions, and all spiritual matter at His feet. The person who wronged us were being used and under Satan's direction, but used by God as an agent to simply show the evil of our own hearts. God has infinite wisdom and He knows exactly what we need to work to get us closer to Him, so He sets the scenes of our lives on His terms.

The key point is, we must praise him anyway, even in the most difficult times. Praise is a discipline God uses to bless us for His glory. Frustration can distract us when our emotions are uncontrolled, that is how the enemy sets up camp in your life. He tries to get you to blame someone else for your troubles, and is the bait of Satan.

Offense is the food for frustration, guilt, resentments and bitterness, blaming others for your lack of praise and your circumstances. It is no one's fault if we seek God's presence on the terms of His authority; we understand the shed blood of our Lord and Savior Jesus Christ. If not at this point, the devil is destroying you spiritually with distractive thoughts of ill feelings of past events, disarming your worship.

We set ourselves up with self-defeating attitudes and behaviors, by doing exactly what God says not to do and then He *will not* use us, but Satan will. It is Satan who will prop us up for defeat; he is the enemy of our soul and wants us to spend eternity with him in hell. We have to stand on God's Word like Daniel, did in the lion's den when faced with attacks, he worshipped God anyway.

It did not matter what the outcome or the distraction was, he kept his focus on God. Daniel's faith in God prepared him, for he decided to stand with God. A word to the wise is that we should make that choice right now and not in the middle of the battle where the enemy is fixed to destroy us.

Make the decision to turn your life and will over to the Lord, for the weapons of your warfare are not carnal but mighty through the Lord to the pulling down of strongholds. By not casting out your vain imaginations, when you shot your spiritual gun to destroy the enemy, you will find no bullets in it; then what?

You are destroyed; a major cause of setbacks in the Body of Christ is our disobedience. God's says that we are soldiers in His army, on a mission to de-populate hell. Find somebody and say do not go to hell by telling them how you came to know the Lord's will help fulfill your life! Worship God on His terms, use the tools of His arsenal be equipped and victorious.

We need on the whole armor of God *(Ephesians 6:11)* to be strong in the Lord and His mighty power. Standing on the Word of God we need the Belt of Truth *(Ephesians 6:14)* to be secured and held tightly in what He has said, which allows us to be freed by the authority of God's Word, and it's mandatory that each Christian has it on.

We trust the Word of God when Jesus said, " *I am the way, the truth and the life" (Matthew 7).* The belt of truth helps us to enter in by the narrow gate, for wide is the gate that leads to destruction and there is many who find it, because *"narrow is the away that leads to life and few find it" (Matthew 7:13).* Are you willing to stand on the Word of

God like the three men in the fiery furnace Shadrach, Meshach, and Abednego? These saints refused to worship anything other than the Most High God, and they were willing to go to the bitter ends to victory. Personal truth is also a notch in the belt of truth, your own honesty and integrity is tested especially when no one sees us.

Ananias and his wife Sapphire died due to the lack of integrity, they lied to the Holy Spirit, and what they perceived as a harmless white lie kill them (Acts 5:1). Have you ever told a harmless white lie? *"There is a way to a man that seems right but the end is always the same death" (Proverbs 14:12)* .

The Word of Truth states *"He who covers sin will not prosper, but who ever confess them and forsake them will have mercy"(Proverbs 28:13).* The next piece of the armor of God is The Breastplate of Righteousness (*Ephesians 6:14).* A solider wears a half -fitted vest on their chest to protect their vital organs. Now the vital organs of the Spirit are Holy living, pure thoughts, action, pure motives and purity of words.

All of which are protected by the Breastplate of Righteousness. On the Sermon on the Mount, Jesus said, *"Ye must be perfect even as your Holy Father is perfect"* (*Matthews 5:48).* Without the worship of God, we don't have a chance against the devil, Paul writes that *"The good things that I want to do I do not do, but the evil things I don't want to do I do" (Romans 7:21).*

Our righteousness is but filthy rags and the enemy knows that. He loves to keep us in bondage by accusing the children of God to be less than what the Lord says they are. The devil is a liar. Without the Breastplate of Righteousness, our hearts are vulnerable and unprotected and we will be defeated.

We protect our hearts with Christ's righteousness, so that we can stand before God justified. As aforementioned, faith without works is dead, we are alive in the Lord, we stay anchored by the guidance of the Holy Spirit, the children of God know His voice and they follow Him. Be kind and compassionate to one another, forgiving each other just as God has forgiven you.

With the Breastplate of Righteousness, we will not compromise our stand on the truth of God's Word. The Breastplate of Righteousness is held tightly to the belt of truth; the connection is that God's Word is secured in our hearts, mind and soul. Do not discount the truth and the authority of the Word of God; it helps us to stand firm in our personal conduct subjected to His will.

God's Word holds us accountable for our every action because the way we live affects other people coming to the Lord. The Breastplate of Righteousness preserves us from the devastating consequences of sin in our lives because the Bible says, *"Set your mind on things above and not on the things of the earth"(Colossians 3:2).*

Our mission is not simply to fight defensively, but offensively; by living a holy life. Satan has won souls by deceit and we must win them back by the truth of the Word of God as soldiers marching into eternity. Our battle is against all darkness and anything that exalts itself above the Word of God proclaiming the Gospel of Jesus Christ. The whole armor of God includes footwear to run, by having "our feet shod with the preparation of the Gospel of peace" *(Ephesians 6:15).*

We must run and tell it by Evangelizing on every mountain, on every hillside and in every valley, on the flat lands, the wet lands and the desert that Jesus Christ is Lord. We have grace in every message of victory, and the peace of mind that Jesus is our Lord and Savior and the battle is already won through Him.

The devil is already defeated what greater assurance is there in each battle we know we can win in Christ. *"For there is but one God and one mediator between God and the people. The man Jesus Christ who gave himself as a ransom for all" (1 Tim 2:5-6).*

We have the peace that surpasses all understanding in knowing we are forgiven and can have a relationship with the Father. We are prepared with the knowledge of the Word of God *"(II Tim 2:15) says, "We must study to show ourselves approved as a workman who is not ashamed and rightly dividing the Word of God".* We're prepared to ex-plain the salvation to others, *"For God so loved the world that He gave His only begotten son so that everyone that believes in Him will not perish but have eternal life" (John 3:16).*

Jesus came so that each of us could know and understand Him in a personal way, so that we would be able to overcome all obstacles and worship Him. Jesus alone can transform our lives if we trust Him and love Him; sold out to Him.

The next piece of armor is the Shield of Faith by which you can extinguish all the fiery darts of the evil one *(Ephesians 6:16).* This piece of armor is essential to those who already believe and trust Christ for their salvation. The flaming arrows of the Shield of Faith quench any attitude that defeats us and causes us destruction.

Satan knows how to hit with a fiery dart such as feelings, thoughts of jealousy, lust, bitterness, unresolved anger, discouragement, grief, worry, despair, and any self-defeating activities. Remember we can do what the devil wants and die, or do what God wants and live. God wants us to live to worship Him in Spirit and in Truth. Be ready to *"walk by faith and not by sight"* *(II Corinthians 5:7),* *"Now faith is the substance of things hope for and the evidence of things not seen" (Hebrews 11:1).*

Have you ever been in a situation when it seemed like everything around you was crumbling and hopeless? It appears to you that it was never going to get better, and one thing after the other just keeps on happening to you. This is when the Shield of Faith protects and breaks all unhallowed grounds.

Remembering how God brought you out with flying colors of past situations; that seemed to be just as hopeless. We must continue to believe that He is loving and caring through the worst storm. Remember the most loving act He could have ever done, He died on the cross in our place for our sins. Remember that God says, *"All things work together for the good of those who love the Lord, who have been called according to His purposes" (Roman 8:28).*

Worship and praise God by your faith and please Him. Trust Him, believe Him, and obey Him in all your acts and ways! The next piece of armor is the Helmet of

Salvation *(Ephesians 6:17);* which awakens the Spirit to the necessity of having a personal relationship with Christ; surrendering your life to Him in faith. Our faith is not in ourselves, or in what we imagine, but in Christ.

The Helmet of Salvation protects us from leaning on our own understanding. Satan will sneak up on us with evil thoughts and offenses in our daily living and especially during worship. He tries to defeat us saying that there is no hope for us, and God will not accept our praise; and this is a big one when he says you are worshiping wrong.

He is cunning and manipulating to fill you with guilt and frustration, to disengage you from the glory of the Lord. He tells you that God will not forgive you as a sinner, do not believe him, he is a liar and the father of them. Having on the Helmet of Salvation, you tell him, "I know who I am and what I am and most importantly, whose I am", therefore, the amour of God quenches the flaming arrows of defeat. Remember that Jesus proved His love for us on Calvary and we are forgiven, and it is no longer what we have done but what He has done for us.

Go ahead, and worship the Lord and praise Him anyway and always trust His promises to us. He is the Lord of all and He cannot lie, so secure your mind to the mind of Christ and what He wants.

Now moving forward to another piece of the whole armor of God, the Sword of the Spirit *(Hebrews 4:12-13),"The Word of God is living and powerful and sharper than any two edged sword piercing to the dividing of the soul and spirit, the joints and marrow, and it is a discerner of the thoughts and intents of the heart. And there is not one thing that is hidden from His sight, but all things are naked and open to the eyes of the Lord who we must give an account of our every action."*

Jesus used the Word of God to refute every temptation of the devil. *"It is written that man cannot live by bread alone, but every Word that precedes out of the mouth of God"* *(Matthew 4:1-11)*. The Word of God is a light giving understanding and guidance from a path of destruction leading us to virtue and trust in God. Trusting God's Word, we are confirmed in Him and His love for us just by believing. *"Your Word is a lamp to my feet and a light to my path" (Psalm 119:105), "The Word of God is like water giving life to a parched earth" (Isaiah. 55:10-11). "The Word of God is like a fire burning in to the soul "(Jeremiah 20:9). "The Word of God is like a mirror that shows us our true condition" (James 1:22-25).*

The Word of God is our lives if only we eat of it with an attitude of there's never enough, the time to build the foundation for your life in the Lord is now. Do not wait, it may be too late, start worshipping God now! Stop! He said now!

Tell yourself "I have to get the worship of God in me" and that my faith in the will, way, and the Word of God is my greatest weapon in the battle against Satan." Through our worship, we acknowledge who God is and we become like Him, snatching our souls back from Hell. Do not allow the enemy of your soul to make you doubt or fear and keep you in bondage, but allow God to deliver you from evil. The Sword of the Spirit will cut all ties from you of darkness. Believe in the truth and the authority of God and come to an understanding of worship, so that you can have an effective walk in Christ. Without the Sword of the Spirit the other pieces of armor are useless, especially the need for prayer which also is a piece of the whole armor of God *(Ephesians 6:18)*.

We are in a battle that we must never surrender or fear being alone. We have fellow believers all over the world and warring holy angels fighting demons in the unseen world. The Holy Spirit is praying for us without ceasing because He knows better than we do what to ask for.

We can have full confidence in approaching God by praying in accordance to His word...*"And this is the confidence that we have in Him, that, if we ask anything according to His will, He hears us: And if we know that He hears us, whatsoever we ask, we know that we have the petition that we desired of Him" (1 John 5: 14-15)*. Pray to God to save us from eternity in Hell, pray for people to know Jesus, pray for people to confess their sins and accept the mercy and forgiveness of deliverance. We unify with other Christians and the angel's of the Lord, defeating the enemy when we pray. Remember not to pray for selfish reasons, but on all occasion for the glory of God. Stay in constant contact with Him every minute of every day. The Word of God is immutable because He cannot lie and we should have strong encouragement of His faithfulness to us as His children; we must be faithful to Him.

We must know and believe that *"The Word of God will not return void unto him but accomplish what it set out to do and will prosper"(Isaiah 55:11).* Belief in the Word of God is true worship and glorifies His excellence. Come into the heart of the Lord of our Salvation praying to invite Him into our lives to change circumstances beyond our human control. Express your love and delight by worshipping the Lord, and be filled with joy! *"I will praise you, O Lord with all my heart; I will tell of all your wonder." (Psalms 9:1).*

EXPRESSIONS OF MY LOVE

Worshiping God is a romance of divine honor,

It is respect and reverence for

the power and position He holds forever.

It is the devotion to His virtue,

for His majesty is sweetness and

His merit is like a lovely fragrance

I long to wear.

In His glory I bathe

in splashing victory.

His mysteries I thirst for

as I meditate on His Word.

My belly is swollen with His promises.

I want to be with Him in the early mornings,

throughout the days and deep into the evening.

I want Him now! In faith, I worship Him,

He is all righteousness.

He caresses me with His love.

He tenderly wipes away my tears.

O' my Lord is coming in the morning to

find me awaken by His voice alone.

My loin's burn with truth for

I am His alone.

His love is mine and will forever be,

He is Love I can see.

His love gives that I may receive.

Silently, I await for Him to pour

His Spirit all over my flesh.

The anointing oil of His Sprit

empowers me; I bask in His peace.

I am limp in surrender,

He revives me and lifts me upon

His shoulder and rejoices.

Oh, Lord I glorify you.

You are my Lord, my Lover, my Priest and my King

Father, touch my soul and call my name.

I will hear you and I follow.

I am the daughter of the Holy One.

Responding to my Master's encompassing love

I sit at the feet of my Lord in

Worship like Mary Magdalene.

I am a devoted servant of God.

Lord, I love you as a lily in the field!

AMEN!

TO GOD BE THE GLORY FOR*EVER!!*

XVI

LET'S SIT AT HIS FEET

AND WORSHIP!

Mary Magdalene was a true worshipper of the Lord Jesus Christ and she holds the distinction of being the first person, and *woman* Jesus Christ revealed himself to after His resurrection. Because of her dark past, her name is often associated with sins of immorality, there is no solid evidence to such conduct; Jesus set her free of seven demons.

She had been tortured by the devil and was undoubtedly afflicted by depression, anxiety, unhappiness, loneliness, self-loathing, shame and fear. Whatever the trouble was, Jesus delivered her and she absolutely worshiped and adored Him. Having been set free from her demons and from sin, she became a slave to righteousness *(Roman 6:18)*. Learning to worship the Lord, Mary Magdalene's example of love and gratitude reflected her commitment to the Lord whom she owed everything to and she knew it.

Mary Magdalene sets a precedent as a woman of God welcomed by Jesus to serve as one of His disciples on His journeys.

We can be assured that all these things were done decent and in order with no reproach. It was unlikely that most rabbis would allow women to serve as disciples. However, Jesus encouraged all to take His yoke and learn of Him.

Mary Magdalene and the other women *"provided for Him from their substance"* according to *(Luke 8:30)*. She supported Jesus and His disciples with her financial resources. Furthermore, her name is at the top of the list of those who worshipped Jesus. She has earned a special place of honor among women; even when Jesus was forsaken by His other disciples, Mary Magdalene remained faithful.

She never left His side when others abandoned Him from Galilee to Jerusalem for the final Passover celebration to the cross and even beyond. Matthew, Mark and John, states that Mary Magdalene was present at the crucifixion with Mary the mother of Jesus, Salome (the mother of apostles James and John), Mary (the mother of James the Less and Joses) and they *"stood by the cross" (John 19:25).*

They heard Jesus commit His mother to the care of John the beloved and as the ordeal of the cross intensified, the women were *"looking on from afar" (Matthew 27:55); Mark 15:4).* The crowd pushed them back, but they remained to the bitter end, powerless to stop the fulfillment of Jesus' assignment. After Jesus gave up the ghost, these women including Mary Magdalene stayed close to the body of Jesus. In fact, it was because of Mary Magdalene (and Mary the Mother of Jesus) the other disciples even knew where to find the body of the Lord (Mark 15:47).

Mary Magdalene's love showed as she took note to where the tomb that they place her Lord in. Jesus had done so much for her and it was heart breaking for her to see the body of her Lord ill prepared. She and the other Mary's planned to give their Master a proper burial worthy of their love and as a final act of worship..."*Now on the first day of the week Mary Magdalene went to the tomb early while it was still dark, and saw that the stone had been taken away from the tomb.* Then she ran and came to Simon Peter, and to the other disciples whom Jesus loved, and said to them " they have taken way the Lord out of the tomb, and we do not know where they have laid Him" (John 20:1).

The Bible further expounds that *"Peter therefore went out, and the other disciple, and were going to the tomb first, and he stooping down and looking in, saw the linen cloths lying there; yet he did not go in. Then Simon Peter came, following him, and went into the tomb; and he saw the linen cloths lying there, and the handkerchief that had been around; His head, not lying with the linen cloth, but folded together in a place by itself. Then the other disciple, who came to the tomb first, went in also; and he saw and beloved. For as yet, they did not know the Scripture that He must rise again from the dead. Then the disciples went away to their own homes. But Mary stood outside by the tomb weeping, and as she wept, she stooped down and looked into the tomb. And she saw two angles in white sitting, one at the head and the other at the feet, where the body of Jesus had lain. Then*

they said to her "Woman why are you weeping?" She said to

them, "Because they have taken away my Lord and I do not

know where they have laid Him"(John 20:1-13).

The women had planned to roll away the great stone

from the mouth of the tomb, but *"a great earthquake"* ac-

complished it (Mathews 28:2). Mary's first thoughts were

that the body of Jesus had been stolen, and she ran to get

help, she met Peter and John on their way to the tomb. She

told them of the empty tomb and they both ran to see for

themselves.

John out ran Peter and stopped at the mouth of the

tomb, but Peter entered into the tomb seeing the empty

grave clothes and headpiece folded and set aside. Then

John came inside the tomb. He also saw the grave clothes

empty, they both believed and they both left (Luke 24:12).

One angel spoke to the women inside of the tomb and said

"He is not here, for He has risen"(Matthew 28:6). He in-

structed them to *"Go quickly and tell His disciples that He*

has risen from the dead" (Matthew 28:7) and *"they went out quickly from the tomb with fear and great joy" (Matthew 28:8).*

Mary remained outside of the tomb distraught over the missing body; she had not notice the empty grave clothes, she did not hear the angel's victorious good news and she did not understand Peter and John's joy upon leaving the tomb.

Then the angel spoke directly to her and ask *"Woman why are you weeping?"* Through her tears she replied, "Because they have taken away my Lord, and I do not know where they have laid Him" (John 20:13). Then Jesus appeared however, she did not recognize Him at all, thinking He was the gardener, she pleaded with Him to show her where He had taken the body of Jesus.

Jesus asked *"Woman why are you weeping? Whom are you seeking? (John 20:15).* She knew His voice and knew then it was Him. *"He calls His own sheep by name and they know His voice" (John 10:3-4). "Rabboni!"* Tears became cheers as she reached out to touch Him (John 20:17) and He told her *"do not cling to me, for I have not yet ascended* *to my Father."*She believed in Him totally; she wanted to hold on to Him forever; a characteristic of a true disciple. Jesus gave to her the honor of seeing Him first after His resurrection. The others heard the good news from angels, but Mary got to hear the news from the mouth of the resurrected Jesus Christ himself.

This was her extraordinary legacy, for her devotion that belongs to no one but Mary Magdalene. We should seek after the Lord and worship Him as she did. We should want to know where He is and follow Him knowing He is worthy and that we owe Him everything. We should want to cling to Him even if we cannot touch Him we should still desire to worship Him in spirit and in truth!

XVII

FACE TO FACE

A true worshipper of the Lord in the intimacy of holiness is face to face with God, and His glory transforms them. Moses experience at the burning bush forever changed him with a new purpose in life. The prophet Isaiah looked up to see the glory of the Lord and he too was changed forever, along with Ezekiel who witnessed God's glory and became the prophet and watchman of Israel.

Each transformation occurred with a vision of the glory of God and the same process goes for us today. When we confessed that God alone can oblige the hunger within, our hearts open to become a worshipper, then we begin to change. He takes away all the barriers in our way that keeps us from Him.

Our spirits witness the glory of the Lord for ourselves, we see the "absolute splendid Holiness of the Lord" and the impact changes our lives forever. We need worship to keep us motivated in our relationship with the Lord. It keeps the fire of our hearts burning vibrantly, no matter what storm we may find ourselves. Worship lifts up our spirits into the arms of the Lord. Moreover, even though we may be suffering, we still worship.

When balanced with the knowledge of our covenant with the Lord, worship makes the following promise a reality *"But in all these things we overwhelmingly conquer through Him who loved us"(Romans 8:37).* The Apostle Paul offers a leading illustration of such an overcomer, who experienced a sweeping change.

With the flawed enthusiasm of a legalistic Pharisee, Saul sought permission from the highest Jewish officials to persecute believers. One day on the road to Damascus, he had an experience that blinded him for three days (Acts 9:3-6).

He was changed spiritually forever when he met the resurrected Jesus! Three days of darkness marked the beginning of the lifetime of open-minded worship for Paul. From that time on, even in the midst of the most horrendous difficulties, he kept the faith and wrote a large part of the New Testament. Paul wrote with confidence because he had learned the truth for himself *"I am more; in labors more abundant, in stripes above measures, in prison more frequent, in death oft. In weariness and painfulness, in watching often, in hunger and thirst, in fasting often in cold and nakedness" (II Corinthians 11:23 b, 27).*

Amazing, that despite all the tribulations of his life, Paul still praised God, *"Rejoice evermore" (I Thessalonians 5:16).* Wherever the Lord told him to walk whether over mountains or through valley's Paul remained a true worshipper producing rich, abundant fruit wherever he went.

As we learn to glorify the Lord in our worshipping, we progress from glory to glory. We'll discover what it really means to abide in God's presence; the Holy Spirit will bring forth fruit in us also, *"The fruit of the Holy Spirit are love, joy, peace, longsuffering, gentleness, goodness, faith, meekness, temperance" (Galatians 5:22,23).* There is a condition in order for us to bear fruit...we must follow the order of the decree. Jesus said *"I am the vine, you are the branches; he who abides in Me and I in him, he bears much fruit; for apart from Me you can do nothing. If you abide in*

Me, and my Words abide in you, and whatever you wish and it shall be done for you. By this is My Father glorified, that you bear much fruit, and prove to be My disciples."(John 15:5,7,8) .

The spiritual makeover in us is like finding an ordinary stone and putting it into the hands of a master sculptor, and it becomes a transformation of art. The Lord can see the saint in the heart of sinners, and as we abide in the Master's plan, the Holy Spirit brings forth the masterpiece for His glory.

We have a great responsibility to remain in the freedom call of holiness. It was not until after God told Moses to build a tabernacle that the blueprint for true worship was birthed, then He spoke *"You shall be holy, for I the Lord your God am holy"(Leviticus 19:2).*

The Lord knew that the Israelites could never be holy unless they learn to worship, and neither can we. As God brings us into holiness, we will fail, but He can still use periods of reversal to develop character. We must see these times as periods of growth and have patience and endurance. We must live above our circumstances to know our sorrow is joy. Depending on God to do the work in us, our lives will become pleasing in His sight. There are immense rewards in minor setbacks. Seeing shortcomings in ourselves is not the end, but the beginning of a newly found treasure. We can take stock in God's faithfulness and draw nearer to *Him in "His presence is fullness of joy and His right hand there are pleasures forevermore!" (Psalm 16:11).* The fuel of worship is a true revelation of the magnitude of the Lord.

The fire that makes the fuel burn white-hot is the quickening of the Holy Spirit. The furnace made alive and warm by the flame of truth is our renewed spirit; the resulting heat of our affections is powerful worship, pushing its way out of confessions, longings, praise, tears, songs, shouts, bowed heads, lifted hands and obedient lives.

Praise God! Worship accomplishes great things for God, both in and through the believer, but we fight a tremendous battle to do it. Why has Satan been taken to the depths to distort the truth of this glorious encounter and distract us from it? Why has he tried to disarm believer's enthusiasm about coming into the Holies of Holy? Simple, he knows the power of worship. Think about it, before Lucifer fell from heaven, he was the worship leader.

When the Body of Christ begins to worship the Father as He intends, there will be the greatest movement of the Holy Spirit the world has ever seen. The Word promises that when the Bridegroom returns to receive His Bride, the Church and she will be spotless. Through perfect love, worship, based on knowledge, and leading to covenant, God's Will, *will* be done in us.

Speaking honestly, we all can use a refresher course on how to appreciate this gift of God. We need to learn to respond to our masters like puppies, with open gratitude, and energetic expectations, eager to please Him. How does the world view us? Can they see that the love for God is our motivator? Do we burn like lights in a darkened world? Worshippers not only burn but they glow. Worship is giving back to God what He has so freely given to us in a spirit of thankfulness.

We present Him a gift for who He is and what He has done because *"The Lord has done great things for us; whereof we are glad" (Psalms 126:3)*. What do you give a man who has everything? He owns the earth in its fullness, what more is left? The greatest thing we can present to God is us and our free will. The Hebrew priest offered sacrifices in the tabernacle, Jesus offered himself as the final sacrifice on the cross; we're not our own we've been brought with a price.

He wants us to come willing to be washed in the blood of the Lamb of God, and filled with His Holy Spirit; consecrated to serve Him. Paul wrote in Romans that this kind of sacrifice leads not to physical death as it did for JESUS, but to a totally new creature of service for the Lord, *"I beseech you brethren, by the mercies of God that ye present your bodies a living sacrifice, holy and acceptable to God, which is our reasonably service" (Roman 12:1)*.

Moreover, in other words being careful not becoming "So heavenly minded that we're of no earthly good." Mountaintops of praise and worship enable us to return to the valleys and be loving servants, a requirement of the Shepherd's Seat Experience. We are not able to love one another unless we first practice loving God.

We cannot reach out for the lost except we see them as God sees them, so we must learn to know Him and to know His is to grow spiritually. As we allow the Lord to develop our heart as true worshippers, we become more like Jesus, who said *"Whosoever will be great among you, you shall minister; and whosoever of you will be the chiefest, shall be servant of all. For even the son of man came not to be ministered unto, but to minister, and to give His life a ransom for many"(Mark 10:43-45).*

Effective Christian service flows from the rivers of living water of their hearts. They acknowledge the glory, majesty and power of our Lord, the King, who came to serve. When we truly love the Lord and want to serve Him, we will not have to break into the Throne room; it's just there in us. Obedience is better than sacrifice and our spirits will exude the joy of salvation in all our work. The King of service will empower us to worship in all that we do, which helps us to desire to go further in the Lord, *"then the joy of the Lord is our strength" (Nehemiah 8:10)*. As our fruit ripen and we grow into maturity, we are freed.

We don't experience the distresses of the world like the world does. The anointing of the Lord softens every blow of life's difficulties. We're not held down in defeat by fear and frustration; we are not like robots, just doing something because it looks good. We are on fire for the Lord filled with genuine love coming from a pure heart.

Service can't replace worship, but it is the outcome of it. We have attitudes of gratitude; when one moves we all move and we worship God first; then we serve others. That is the divine order God has ordained, Jesus did things with divine order during His temptation in the wilderness. He told Satan, *"Get the hence, Satan: for it is written, thou shall worship the Lord thy God, and Him only shall thou serve" (Matthew 4:10)*.

Worship is who you are, where you are as an expression of love and gratefulness, in response of the goodness of the Lord. It's the work of our heart, not with the fleshy desires or even its blessing, but only God alone. This means referring to ourselves in humility like King David did after he learned what great things were planned for him, *"And what can David say more unto thee? For thou, Lord God knows thy servant. For thy Word's sake, and according to thine own heart, hast thou done all these great things to make thy servant know them. Wherefore thou art great, O Lord God for there is no one like thee, neither is there any God beside thee according to all that we have heard with our ears"* (*II Samuel 7:20-22*).

We have to be still long enough for God to create a clean heart in us. Any other form of service turns out to be counterfeit, it's not real; by identification, the work done by a worshipper will have eternity in it. Yes, we can make up fake ministries to further our own selfish ambitions and we deceive ourselves and put up a counterfeit light around us for people to see. We put on a beautiful covering to hide the old inner man's hateful self, and with no heart work done on a daily basis, there lacks the sincerity of God's love. God makes perfect cakes of righteousness; He doesn't need icing to cover the flaws. When we abide in the Lord we gain the confidence of sincerity all can see, and He, through repentance, He alone keeps us from being polished apples filled with worms. Yes, the real Fruit of the Spirit is love, joy, peace, longsuffering, gentleness, meekness, and temperance, grown only in the abundance of God.

We've been equipped as believers with everything we need to serve the Lord. We don't have to work on our own agenda, He has supplied His. We are the fruitful branches of the love of God, reaching out into the world and changing it. We need the power of the Spirit of the Lord to worship and serve Him, we cannot do it alone. God has commissioned us to save the world, through the anointing and the gifts of the Holy Spirit.

The Church has one head and that is Jesus, *"And He is the head of the body, the church; who is the beginning, the firstborn from the dead; that in all things He might have the preeminence"(Colossians 1:18).* For the shepherding and perfecting of His body, Jesus established certain spiritual offices, commonly known as the "fivefold ministry." Paul catalog them in his letter to the Ephesians Church, the Apostle, Prophet, Evangelist, Pastor and Teacher.

Not everyone has a pastor's call, but, we can be assured that God has called each of us to serve and equipped us with at least one spiritual gift to make up for our weaknesses.

"Now there are diversities, but the same Spirit. And there are differences of administrations, but the same Lord. And there are diversities of operations, but it is the same God, which worketh all in all. But the Manifestation of the Spirit is given to every man to profit withal. But all these worketh that one and the selfsame Spirit, and dividing to everyman severally as He will (I Corinthians 12:4-7,11). For as we have many members in one body and all the members do not have the same office, so we, being many, are one body in Christ, and every one members one of another. Having then gifts differing according to the grace given to us, let each prophesy according to the proportion of faith" (Roman 12:4-6). We are all bounded together by God, but we do

not become "copy cats" of one another. The Lord has ordained our roles. He helps each of us become fruitful in the ministry for the Lord.

When the world sees the Church, we must effectively and forcefully look like we belong to the Lord. We worship in the Spirit of God and the glory in Christ Jesus and put *"no confidence in the flesh" (Philippians 3:3).*

The verse...by my Spirit, says the Lord of Hosts, reminds us that lifestyle of worship fills up the wellspring from which loving, dynamic Christian service flows. No more feelings of being driven to labor, so we can rest with clear consciences. Rather, service rises out of the deepest beings in gratitude to the precious Lord.

Rejoice in the communion of the Lord, the wellspring of life. We can be confident that God will fulfill everything He said in His promises through us. Thank you Lord, we can breathe easy because it's true, the Holy Spirit is preparing us to stand before the Lord in total awe of His splendid glory. Our heads should bobble with the spectacular thought of standing in total silence of the glory of the

Lord. It is a Godly fear that grabs hold of our bellies and squeezes it again and again; don't be afraid to worship the Lord.

We must honor the Lord and the work He has given us to do now in preparation of a day to come when the angels stop saying, "HOLY, HOLY, HOLY. We catch a glimpse of Jesus as both the sacrificial Lamb and the soon coming King. We witness, with the Apostle John, the immeasurable thousands worshipping the Father and Son in the most superb service ever to be gathered.

The Holy Spirit wants to unveil yet one scene in our heavenward gaze, the demonstration that will take place at the beginning of God's judgment. *"And when He broke the seventh seal, there was silence in heaven for about half an hour (Revelation 8:1).* A holy stillness will settle over heaven! Think of that, for the first time since God spoke the universe into being, angelic mark of respect will cease.

No more cries of, "Holy, Holy, Holy!" ringing forth from the throne room. No more heavenly exaltation accompanying the saints praises. An absence of sound will saturate the universe. *"Be still and know that I am God"* *(Psalm 46:10)*, this will be the fulfillment of this Psalm. Everything in heaven, in earth, and under the earth, yes the devils will be silent too. God the Father will rise from His Throne to pronounce judgment, for an half hour, every eye will be engrossed on Him, silenced by His inconceivable glory.

An indication to this fundamental event appears in another Psalm *"Thou didst cause judgment to be heard from heaven; the earth feared and was still, when God arises to judgment, to save all the humble of the earth (Psalm 76:8,9).* Later, the Lord revealed to the prophet Daniel the wonders that'll follow, *"I beheld and the same horn made war with the saints, and prevailed against them; until the Ancient of days came, and the judgment was given to the saints of the most High and the time came that the saints possessed the kingdom" (Daniel 7:21,22).*

After God the Father stands.

He'll assume His rightful place on the

Throne Of Judgment.

"I kept looking until throne were set up, and the ancient of Days took His seat; His vesture was like white snow. And the hair of His head like pure wool, his throne was ablaze with flames, it's wheels were a burning fire. A river of the fire was flowing and coming out from before Him; thousands upon thousands were attending Him, and myriads upon myriads were standing before Him. The court sat, and the books were opened"(Daniel 7:9-10).

Silent, awesome, deafening, QUIET! This is the most incredible thing I have ever known, the idea of being in absolute silence about to be judged; spirit quickens into humbleness. I am in awe of the power of the Lord. It makes my heart shake with repentance. What will it be like for our ears to hear everything muted by His power? God is not playing and it's time to stop playing.

The mighty move of God is at hand, and soon the silence at the throne. I want my eyes blameless on Him, looking at Him in every way. I want to follow His movements with my eyes, as He stands to pronounce the living and the dead. No one will miss this day, we will see Him as

He is and the Lord is calling now. He is right here now for us to worship and obey in Spirit and in Truth. Let us stand together in the unity of faith as one with Him in the silence.

The Lord is more than powerful; words are not enough to explain the awesome might of Him who will settle all disputes. So great is our magnificent Lord of heaven, that incalculable numbers will be speechless before Him. The Holy Spirit is moving on our behalf to prepare us for that day when time is drawing closer. He longs to teach us to worship in gracious wonder, in high-spirited gratitude.

We have the opportunity of the ages and God gives us freedom to choose. How wise He is. We can run eagerly into His loving clutch or turn our backs on Him. Make up your mind the choice is still yours. Get to know Him before the silence, and I believe it will happen in this generation. Amen!

XVIII

RAISE LEADERS IN THE KINGDOM

God's Kingdom will come and His Will shall be done. Our Lord is such an awesome Lord. He loves us so much; our hearts are too small to hold the love He called us to receive. He expects each of us to come into the totality of our purpose in Him. God means for each of us to become leaders and the Holy Spirit is working to do just that.

Our feelings of inadequacy causes us to stumble and it blocks our development. And if that weren't enough, it also blocks the growth and development of the Kingdom of God in His people. We have to recognize that God has called us to move higher and higher and He is looking for people just like Him.

He will not accept anything less than the very best. They must have the same vision as God has for the people. It is important for each of us to understand our role in the Body of Christ. Then we can stop telling everyone else what their places is and step up to the plate by not just being in church; but the church being in you. Many are called into the fivefold ministry and they must walk in the office as God has called them.

A great responsibility goes intimately with God's calling which holds them accountable before the Lord on how they ministered the sheep He gave them. *"God resists the proud" (James 4:6),* and He rejected King Saul and chose David to be the King because of it. God is merciful but He will reject the proud, how far do we go for God to reject us?

God is not going to put up with leaders who are proud and He will set himself against them. Repent now in the name of Jesus and become Kingdom minded. Saul was not Kingdom minded, he was strictly concerned with his own empire. He was out for himself and fought to keep the reign and lost everything, including his mind, trying to hold on to what he wanted. He was known to be a leader who did not have the heart for the people and this is true today. For this very reason, we see so many people running from church to church hurt and bleeding.

Leaders are not sensitive enough to their needs and no healing and deliverance takes place; God's people have been misguided. God is raising up leaders in His Kingdom, trained and instructed by the Holy Spirit. Leaders who show true love and are willing to reach out and touch the Body of Christ with divine concern. They will be willing to train other leaders in the church investing time to teach and preach the Word of God.

They will be willing to give all of themselves to help expand the Lord's word throughout the earth. Persecuted and rejected by other leaders after their own selfish ambitions, they will be left to die in the storm, but God has hidden them in the secret place of His will.

The church needs leaders who understand their callings and who operate at the most excellent state. Leader, who have the willingness to do what God said to do.

This is the highest and most blessed aspect of the Shepherd's Seat Experience. We are in a season of perfection and the Body of Christ is in the season of transformation. Moreover, like the butterfly who knows instinctively that a change is about to occur, God has placed us in our perspective places to grow into more than what we are now.

Within the cocoon of the Body of Christ, the worm forms a cocoon to begin its process of metamorphosis. The insect knows that it was not to be designed to crawl forever, but to soar like an eagle high in the sky. This is a revelation for all Christians: the cocoon is either a sanctuary or a prison. It's decreed by the attitude you have toward its processing. It will also determine how long you will be in any give process.

Imagine the muffled cries of a caterpillar in its cocoon, that would be very unnatural and it is not what God ordained. Be quiet and stop complaining about "going through" and go through, things will be less difficult. Murmuring and complaining makes, our problems seem bigger. Start praising God for whatever He has wrapped you in for a particular season and you will emerge like the butterfly totally transformed by God. God is trying to get us off our belly crawling and set us free to go up higher.

God is releasing a harvest of butterflies in His service only who have been liberated from past difficulties to give us a future of freedom. He has a better place for us to go all the time, so stop trying to break through the old skins of your cocoon on your own.

There is no other way, "Except the Lord build the house, they labor in vain that build it: except the Lord keep the city, the watchman wakes but in vain" (Psalm 127:1). Get busy working in the Kingdom of God and He will bless you with His harvest. The harvest is truly plentiful, but the laborers are few *"Therefore pray the Lord of the harvest to send out laborers into His harvest" (Matthew 9:37-38).* People are the harvest and until our leader's eyes are opened to see the harvest the way that Jesus sees it, they cannot operate the way Jesus operates.

He told us to pray to the Lord of the harvest so that He would send laborers into His harvest. This is not a harvest of prosperity of mammon; it's the prosperity of souls for the Kingdom of the Lord. I pray that the Lord will send out many laborers to harvest the ripened souls for the work in the ministry. Do not be surprised if you find yourself in a completely different operation, as God moves in your life that you will move in other's lives.

You are about to be ejected from the complacency you have to set up in your personalized cocoon. He is serving eviction notices throughout the Body of Christ. You have been sitting in the church going nowhere and it is time to move into the required destiny of the Lord. God is about to give you your wings.

You are going to find yourselves in the community where the souls are dying. The Shepherd's Seat Experience is all about doing the will of God. Souls belong to Him, and if someone had something that belongs to you, would you not go get it too?

God is coming for His souls; He's preparing His souls for the harvest. Ripened fruit are waiting to be picked by the laborers of the Lord. God is sending us in to the market place to go get what belongs to Him. There is a powerful anointing like never before on these men and woman in Leadership going forth. The devil cannot stop them; they have experienced suffered and are not afraid to stand rooted and grounded, decreeing and declaring the Word of the Lord. He will use them mightily to bring in the harvest, to manifest His glory for all to see.

Ask God for a revelation to the importance of the commitment it will take to accomplish this work. God is launching them right in the devil's territory, ready to do warfare. The devil is not just going to sit back and let us freely do anything, he'll attack and try to send us back hiding in the church.

The devil is a liar and do not expect for this warfare to decrease, it'll by all means increase. The Lord of the harvest has sent us forth; His heart is for the harvest. Get a mirror, go ahead!

I mean, it is very important that you understand this point about the Shepherd's Seat Experience. Now look at yourself in the mirror and say, "I'm the harvest hands God has chosen to pick fruit" it is all for the glory of the Lord. Our hands will not be empty, God has given us great power and authority to do this work, Matthew 10:1 says

"He gave them power over unclean spirits, to cast them out, and to heal all kinds of sickness and all kinds of disease."

We should be in prayer concerning this harvest asking God to help us continue the work that Jesus gave the twelve disciples. He equipped them and then gave them power and authority to establish the Church. Now, it is our turn to take the reins of this authority and go in the name of Jesus to the field gathering the harvest of souls waiting on the glory of the Lord.

"In the beginning", God gave Adam and Eve dominion and then they gave it to the devil. Again, the devil is a liar; and we are taking it back in the name of Jesus. We are supposed to send out sons and daughters of the Lord to do just that. God's plans have not changed; this is the same process we'll use to establish the Kingdom of the Lord.

Leaders must stop being afraid to raise up children and let them go. They do not belong to you, they are the disciples of Jesus. We must equip them with every necessary tool that is available to us. This is how we multiply on the earth, it is not the size of our congregations, it's the quality of our congregations that count. We measure by the leaders we raised up and trained in the way they should go.

We release the likeness of Jesus all over the planet earth working not only for today but working for eternity. We are servants of God who must reproduce ourselves through our ministry and give our spiritual children the authority that God gave us. We provide the foundation for success for the generations to come.

The fivefold ministry leaders must release authority, and the members within the Body of Christ must be willing to accept it. Jesus paid a high price for us and we yield to the work we were redeemed to do.

LESSON

Thank God, for Jesus made the final transaction for our freedom. Rise up O mighty nations thus says the Lord *"The twelve Jesus sent out..."(Matthews 10:5).* "Sent" means *apostello* in Greek and it means to be a "sent one" on a mission. We are all called to be sent out in the name of Jesus according to the Great Commission in Matthews 28.

God is removing people off the pews, and putting them in the fields to take the Gospel to the world, *"As you sent me into the world, I also have sent them into the world" I do not pray for these alone, but also for those who believe in me through my Word" (John 17:18,2).* God is an apostolic God who sent His Son Jesus.

Jesus sent the Holy Ghost, and the Holy Ghost is sending the Church (us) into the world. Go and tell the world about Jesus and all the wonderful things that He has done. You are not acting alone and fear will not overtake you. Keep on moving and pressing towards the mark of the high calling in Christ Jesus. (Philippians 3:14).

You are commissioned to do a specific work for a specific reason and you have been equipped to do the work. Go ahead and step into your destiny on your own or fall into it through error. One way or the other you will do what God purposed you to do. If we gather in the church that is good, but it's the scattered church that matters. God is bringing His original plan for the church into its proper position; to turn the world upside down *"Those who were scattered went everywhere preaching the Word. Then Phillip went down to the city of Samaria and preached Christ to them. And the multitudes with one accord heeded the things spoken by Phillip, hearing and seeing the miracles which he did" (Acts 8:4-6).*

God's vision is not to fill the church with people, it is to take the entire world for God. Come on people of God, get up out of your seats and go conquer the world for the Lord. The call for evangelism will hit your bellies hard with a burning on your lips with the Word of God.

I don't know what your plans were, but they have been changed. Stay actively praying to God for the good works of the Kingdom to manifest every place He sends you, take over the world with the Gospel.

Use the gifts and authority to take back the grounds the devil has stolen by deceit. Depopulate hell and bring in the harvest of the souls God has ordained from the very beginning. Go ahead and get busy being in the army of God. Take off those flimsy garments of the flesh and put on the full armor of God. God is releasing His army to be prepared for these last days encounter of hell. Be willing to give all that you have to keep what belongs to God, we have total and absolute victory, the devil is defeated.

The anointing of God is on you right now! This is an exhilarating time to live; God is pouring His Spirit out over the world. Keep praying and aligning yourselves with the army of the Lord. Each of us is welcome to this out-pouring. You are blessed to be a blessing; pass it on and give what was so freely given to you in the name of Jesus Christ; get busy!

"If my people who are called by my name, will humble themselves, and pray and seek my face, and turn from their wicked ways, then I will hear from heaven, and will forgive their sin and will heal their land"(II Chronicles 7:14). Look at the gifts God has given you and allow Him to perfect them in you.

Don't try to do anything that God didn't ordain you to do or condemn yourself for what you were not called to do. God has personally given you a particular task and service to perform and that is all that is required of you to complete. Do not despise the small things that God has you to do; He is watching to see if you truly belong to Him. Do not make things hard on yourself; trust God and His infinite wisdom, to rocket you through this dark times into the light forever.

What you have not been called to do you ca not do. Stop wasting time and get on track with the Lord. Again, I say rejoice in the Lord and praise Him for the work He has already performed.

IXX

MY TESTIMONY

I want to be the best that God has made me to be. It seems hard sometimes to see how the world treats you. Also as a woman in the ministry, coming into contact with some of the members of the Body of Christ who can hurt you far worse than the world ever could. It's devastating to know that the Saints are not such good leaders or examples.

Thank you God, for the many great and anointed men and women who do honor their office and leadership, and are rightly joined to it. A Leader must be willing to lay down His life for his sheep. As a chosen vessel, I declare my desire is to minister and motivate the people to reach their fullest capabilities. God has placed in my heart the gift of love and warm friendship.

I'm blessed to want to give it away and I desire to help the people learn to be disciplined in God. I love to hear the praise reports of what God is doing in the lives of the Saints. I see the Kingdom of God rising in every face. I won't live in a box or minister from one; God is not limited and I have faith in the Lord for the great work ahead of leading people to be saved.

I am so ecstatic in the ministry, and I want to do all the things that the world said I could not do. I can do all things through Christ who strengthen me and I am a witness to the goodness of the Lord. I give Him all the glory for He has never left in the same condition; even from a minute ago. He's always moving and so should the leadership developing in our churches.

Without Jesus, I'm nothing and I need the Lord to show me how to do everything. I love talking to Him, crying to Him and worshipping Him in the best way I know how. The great thing about the Lord is, once I'm developed in one level, He gives me another. This experience of finding out who God is manifests itself in the character of who our leaders are.

I want the Holy Spirit to run, to overflow in the Body of Christ and set the saints on fire. I want that fire in me, I can feel the heat rise inside of me. Holy Ghost fire is what the Body of Christ is calling for. As a leader, I must know why I'm leading; I know that God called me to do this work, and He gave me a gift of commitment to achieve it. I humble myself at the feet of the King; expressing that I know nothing and am nothing without the direction of His Holy Spirit.

I have a desire to train the people and release them to go out and do the same. It's the only way the Kingdom will be established on earth by releasing leaders to make leaders. My future lies in the relationship I have with the Lord. The Shepherd's Seat Experience is all about the glory of The Lord. It's all about the knowledge He will impart inside of our hearts.

It's all about drawing us near to Him, but it is our choice to do so. It is all about learning the blessings of the Lord by knowing the Lord. It's all about the love that God shows His children. It's God's dedication and authority to inspire us to keep going higher. I see myself in this high place, a place that has already been occupied by God. It's magnificent and glorious as the Lord himself, who owns all the wonders here. I belong to God and I'm a wonder here also, because He didn't have to let me in, but He did. I am blessed, knowing that God has allowed me entrance into this gate of beauty.

The beauty is the heart of God; the knowledge that it opens for each of us staggers my whole being. God, absolute and marvelous, stands and He's the mountain, the high place I am attached to in His presence. It's the glory of the Lord that has provided the excellence to release me and to train me by His Holy Spirit.

It's the heart of God that I have traveling mercies to enter in and grow to the four winds with His revelations. With the revelations that are pouring into my spirit, I realize that there are not enough words to express the great and faithful God that surrounds me all in all.

It's amazing that because of the Holy Spirit, I made it through a world who hates me because I'm saved, I made it through "church folks" who judged me and I made it through my own self-righteousness to rejoice in the success of the Kingdom of the Lord. I know that I'm not my own and that I belong to the Lord. God is with me through the difficult times and He's my help, He teaches me to stand in His presence without fidgeting with confidence.

I'm a leader because God says I am. Even if no one follows me, I lead myself in obedience. I never set out to find a way to glorify God; He made a way out of no way, and I have a victorious life; I didn't do it; God did it. I want what God wants for His people; to love them and give all that I have spiritually.

I believe the church is filled with leaders who haven't been trained by the Holy Spirit. I did not say they don't have the Holy Spirit, they have not allowed Him to teach them. A leader is a person who has the ability to help others succeed; they are holy and righteous. They push the people forward and expect nothing in return because they have been taught by the Holy Spirit.

Let's encourage one another and lift up goodness, mercy and stop letting evil rein in *any* area of our lives. The attitudes of our hearts makes a difference in this unholy world; our character should be humble, and our heart developed by God's Word, Way, and Will, to show us what should not be there. Try to become a better person through others; it is very important to other human beings with love. It is about showing them that God is presence in your life through love and friendship. I want what's best for my fellowman and I am to train others to follow this same precept.

It took a while to understand, but it is not always the devil defeating us, it's sometimes our own human spirit opposing the Will of God. I admire David greatly, because the Bible says, he had a heart after God's own heart. WOW, that is quite an achievement, and he accomplished it by having a repenting heart. Repenting is like running fresh clean water through a clogged up drain.

It cleans it and then the water can move freely. True repentance will reach out to forgive in humility, to make things right before the Lord. Cleansing the clogged drains of our heart imposes a sanction of purity in the eyes of the Lord. It brings the blessing of God's favor upon us. Now I say...Lord I repent, I'm so sorry for my wrong doings, please forgive me; and I feel better? I do! If we operate with clean hearts as Leaders, we are kind and considerate of others.

We don't demand ungodly things of people because we don't want people to fall. Sometimes we may demand a set standard of holiness, but not maliciously, and with a desire for people to grow. We can even cause ourselves to stumble, but God understands and knows our heart, so we keep on doing better.

God will show us the right way, however it still doesn't excuse our behavior; again it's a process, and we are all learning. If any leader thinks that they have arrived, that have not. We all fall short of the glory of the Lord (Romans 3:23). We all make mistakes and we must help one another to do better next time. Jesus said *"Learn of me for I am meek and lowly in heart" (Matthew 11:29).*

The Lord said, "learn" to be meek. Sometimes we don't see our own faults and expect others to accept it because we are in leadership. Not so, as leaders, we are striving to be like Christ even more so than others. We have to be hungry and thirsty for the Lord's Word. We must show mercy in God's goodness as we walk upright before the Lord and He always shows mercy.

The people we lead should believe goodness and mercy are following them all the days of their lives. A pure heart and pure eyes sees God. I am not just speaking of the future, but seeing God today. This is a leader who walks holy in heart, attitude and body and is led by God's Spirit. Peace is what I seek.

I try to go out of my way to walk in love with people, with clean hands. I am interested in the very best for those around me, and this is often the most painful area because so many people have no expectation in the Lord. Many of these people get hurt easy and run from church to church until that leader pushes their button again.

It is a spiritual pattern that I have observed in people that say they love the Lord but want to do things their way. It is not because they do not have a loving and caring leader, but because they do not trust the Lord's choices for them. However, many times they have just cause to run for their lives, but we still have to learn to be content in whatever state we find ourselves until God releases us. It is important to keep communicating with people to find a happy medium, as a leader this is not a choice, but a must.

Nevertheless, I realize that no matter what you do people may not see what God has right in their faces, and will run in a blink of an eye. As leaders, we should have the ability to bring peace to troubled people. It is God's peace and is available to us all; we should not be hurt when people do not receive it, but we are. If that is the case, we have to mature in this area without getting an old crusty heart of rejection.

When the path to peace is established with people, then peace can be found on a personal basis. Trusting God's unchanging hand is peace and always acting right and doing right in the middle of being wronged. God must have complete control in the lives of His people. Hold on even if it hurts, especially if it hurts, and He will heal you. God inducts us into the Kingdom and trains us in every area of our lives. We have to be opened to all the details that the Holy Spirit will reveal to us and be ready to change it.

Take a hold of the sin nature living inside of you by the neck and make it bow down to the Lord Jesus Christ. Everything that we endeavor must be done by the power of the Holy Spirit. Our ministries are birthed through prayer and we must stay before God to represent God to our congregation and staff.

Through prayer, we preach, teach and shepherd the sheep. Through prayer, a true dependency on God is revealed. God wants us to learn to get lost in the spirit of prayer. He wants us to examine our hearts; and to look for His presence in our character, in and out of the pulpit. *Examine your heart as a Leader in the Kingdom,* are you receiving revelation? Are you tried and tested?

Do you share your authority? Are you of a broken and contrite spirit? Are you a true shepherd? Are you rational? Are you called by God? Are you motivated? Are you compassionate? Are you a lover of God's people? Are you consistent? Are you an exhorter? Are you filled with courage? Are you a giver? Are you secure in who you are? Are your goals Christ center? The best way to lead people is to take them down the same path that you went. To teach them the things that you have learned in Christ. Build leaders who are prepared for the last day church.

This church is built upon the Kingdom agenda and not flimsy personalities or ministries. God is looking for people who love Him and who wants to follow wherever He wants to take them. God wants us to stand up together as His people.

This is the day of the righteous people rising against the gates of hell. This is all the plan of God and man had not one thing to do with it. He has set it in motion for a specific purpose and the Holy Spirit is overseeing the activity on earth, the purpose is stated *"Go ye" (Matthew 28:19)*. The Body of Christ will fulfill its destiny that God ordained for us. It's time to train soldiers in the army of the Lord, time for just tending the sheep is up *"And He himself gave some to be Apostles, some Prophets, some Evangelists, and some Pastors and teachers for the equipping of the* saints for the work of the ministry, for the edifying of the Body of Christ (Ephesians 4:12-12).

Time is up for playing church. It is time to rock and roll in the Spirit of God. It is His music I hear, playing a tune of the trump of God soon to be released. It is a time for us to join hands in the unity of faith. We must reach out to our brothers and sisters in Christ and say let's do this work.

God wants to put to a stop people running back and forth from church to church-looking for a prophet to give them a word. Get your own word! God wants us to link with a good home church and be trained and equipped with God's purpose. Stop wasting time looking for a church whose leaders fit your "must have" list and the choir of your liking.

Look for the move of God and a leader moved by God working to perfect the saints, to do the work of the ministry, to edify the Body of Christ. It is not about the celebrity leader; who is that person if they are not truthfully God's material? God said He would pour His Spirit on all flesh and not just the leaders you think. You will be disappointed repeatedly. We have to allow God to show us where to go and what leaders we need to have as our shepherds.

Stop placing leaders on pedestals that is just setting them up to fall, but do honor and have respect for them as your overseer and a follower of Christ themselves. God is the one who makes vessels of men and women of God and the power is in Him only. Without God, we are nothing. It grieves the Holy Spirit when we take our eyes off the work He does and give it to mortal men or women.

It is by God's authority that we are called into the ministry; He appoints to serve Him. Praise God! He set up the church for His glory to manifest on earth. We honor our leaders; but we do not place them above the power of the Lord. The Body of Christ is moving into a new season of God's anointing. It is the season for the harvest *"In due season we shall reap, if we faint not" (Galatians 6:9). "To everything there is a season" (Ecclesiastes 3:1).* The Shepherd's Seat Experience has taken me from sitting on a mountain in the Spirit; to finding out the mountain was

God. I was not to sit but to bow down and worship Him for He is the Almighty God. Through this work, I have been enlighten and blessed with power I did not have when I first began. I have obtained a greater knowledge of the things pertaining to the Lord; specifically the perfecting of the saints, the work of the ministry and the edifying of the Body of Christ.

I have found faith waiting on the Lord, after much effort learning to wait on Him and to operate in the gifts solely for His purposes. I am caught up in the awe of knowing that God personally set it up for me to discover, I am not my own. God is my maker and He is in control of our making. The revelation is that God called leaders out of the valley and prepares them to return for the edifying of the Body of Christ.

He leads us down a path of righteousness for His namesake. That is awesome! I will rejoice in heaven when God gives me more words to express His glory. There are not words on earth to express the way I feel after going through this, and of many Shepherd Seat Experiences.

Gratitude is all over me. I believe that the power of God's authority to go forth; to learn how to love, worship, and return to the Lord is all over me. I perceived that the place God had taken me was a place of aloneness, but not loneliness. God was allowing me my process of returning into His presence forever.

I exist for His glory and His glory alone. I am truly blessed to bless you. Now I am passing this baton to you to start your Shepherd's Seat Experience, already in progress before the foundation of the world. God has established in us a finished work. We will shed every bit of flesh in order to receive our glorified bodies like Christ.

The Shepherd's Seat Experience has bought me from a vision of me in the spirit, to the vision for the Kingdom of God and a harvest of souls. I love you and I pray that you stay plugged into the vision of your house. Take it and release the butterfly of victory to the world. A glorious Church is emerging. Rise and take up your bed and go home! God Bless You! Thank You God!

My Request O God

Help us O God to enjoy The Shepherd's Seat Experience. The wonderful relationship of getting to know who you are. Help us to sit with you and feast with you. Help us to talk to you and to embrace you. May we live our lives in the light of this wonderful relationship and the love that is amassed to us because of it.

It is wonderful to know that you care for us and that you are thinking about us all the time. Even before we think about ourselves, you think *about* us. You already have opened a way for us, so we trust in *you*. Thank you for making us a source of great blessing to others. We pray in the name of *Jesus*. We thank you for the power of the blood of the Lamb and for the guidance of the Holy Spirit. *Amen*

IT IS... FINISHED!

Work Cited

Bevere, J. (2005).*Drawing Near, A Life Journey of Intimacy with God.* Nashville, Tennessee: Thomas Nelson.

Bridges, J. (2006). *The Pursuit of Holiness.*

Gills, J. (1994). *The Dynamics of Worship.*

Hagin, K. (2002). *Understanding the Anointing.*

Lucado, M. (2003). *Experiencing the Heart of Jesus.*

Mac Arthur, J. (2005). *Twelve Extraordinary Women.*

Nance, T. (2005). *God's Armor Bearer.*

Wardle, T. (2005). *The Souls' Journey.*

MORE BOOKS BY DR. MELVA DORSEY

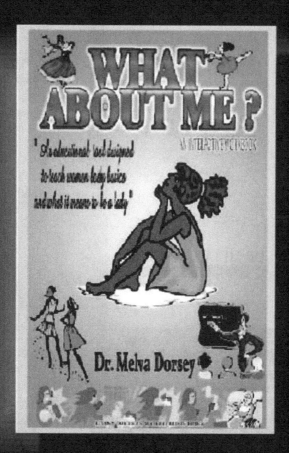

WHAT ABOUT ME?" is a 24 page interactive workbook designed to teach women about their body basics and functions of the female reproductive system. It is a great tool to be used in treatment centers, schools, churches, community centers and in the home. It is benefical for any female from puberty to menopause.

Anointed, Appointed & Approved

The Shepherd's Seat Experience teaches the importance of holiness through the worship of the Lord. In addition, it teaches the Kingdom minded authority needed to edify the Body of Christ. This book demonstrates how we should trust God and live by His promises in faith. Readers will also learn how to face adversities by understanding how God operates through His word. This beneficial book teaches Christians how to sit at the feet of the Lord Jesus Christ in total selflessness. It opens our eyes with the truth of God sovereignty and our feebleness. This book shares the wisdom of God's grace and gives us the peace we need to be worshippers holy and acceptable in the sight of God. This is a powerful piece of armor to help eradicate our free will choice to be the will of God forever and foremost! The Shepherd's Seat Experience opens a way for us to learn to become a source of great blessings to others. The Holy Spirit will help you to understand and apply the instructions of this book to your lives. You will be transformed by the renewal of your mind. You are truly blessed to bless others. The baton has passed into your hands to start your own Shepherd's Seat Experience.

TRUST   TRUTH

Apostle/Prophet of God Dr. Melva Dorsey is the overseer of Living Waters World Ministries located in Cleveland, Ohio. Dr. Melva Dorsey is an anointed Woman of God whose prophetic insight has encompassed holiness to the utmost. She is a global conference speaker with an undeniable call to motivate and encourage others. She is the author of "People of Ashes" and "What About Me?" all to edify the Body of Christ. She is armed with a Kingdom mind dedicated to the Lord! She boldly proclaims the prophetic truth of God's word and is thus sought after grossly! She enjoys life in Cleveland, Ohio with her husband Elder Alvin Dorsey.